WRECKLESSLY ABSURD

True
Funny
Crazy
Stories

CHANCE J.J. EDRIC

Aka
Chance the Author
(not The Rapper)

Positivity Publishing LLC

The mutha fuckin copyright page. Est. 2019

The true names have been protected for security reasons. While the story is always true, identities have been changed as to comfort the unbeknownst family members and general community. Any coincidence of living, actual being is a pure fucking lucky coincidence. Or you have the same dumbass group of buddies that I do (which for that I apologize). Anyways, this is just to point out that there is no need to sue. If there were any true people that shared in the same weird life that I entail in the coming pages, they would all be off the grid and would have all gone underground. They might have even relocated to far off, exotic locations, such as Omaha, Nebraska and Pahrump, Nevada.

This needs to be said though:
Criminal copyright infringement is investigated by the FBI and may constitute a felony with a maximum penalty of up to five years in prison and/or a $250,000 billion dollar fine. If you live in the Russian territory of Russia, you will most likely not see your next birthday. No fine though.

Seriously. I could give two fucks if this gets stolen. Do you know the return on one of these dumbass books? Yeah. It's next to nothing. $1.13 per sold copy. The price I get for someone reading my book? Measured in love and tears. Not actual taxable dollars.

My point is this:
If you are going to "borrow" this through ill gotten, but totally understandable means, the worst you could do is leave an honest (but not too honest) review somewhere that likes reviews. Even Yelp if you absolutely need to. Every bit of social loves helps a starving artist. You are a God's angel for spending any time with me and my crazy life and my imaginary friends.

Steal away, but at least be useful thieves.
Copyrighted February 14th, 2019

Cover Design by James, GoOnWrite.com

Ghost Edited by Freddie Mercury

Really Edited by Mitchell Notes n Shit

Sometimes Edited by Elizabeth's Kindergarten Kids

Proudly NOT Edited by George Carl the Third

Wanted to be Edited by William James Murray (Look for his audio version in late 2019 to 2032'ish)

Publisher's Note

Please note the publisher decided to not note anything about the publishing of this document.

Author's Note

Dad, this is as far as you should read. This is your final warning. For fucks sake Dad, do you really want a heart attack? Because this is how you get one! Mom, please take away the book from dad.

Author's Other Note

If any harm becomes of you while reading the information within these hallowed pages that is of your own fault. I very seriously doubt you can laugh to death. Heart attack? Possible. Maybe you should have put down that last jelly fritter or that 64 oz Fosters. Don't blame me for that. That's just bad manners on your part.

Ordering Information

Go to the internet. Type in "Wrecklessly Absurd" and follow links. If that doesn't work, then try "Chance J.J. Edric" and see what pops up. If that doesn't work, then turn off your computer or phone and turn it back on. Then try the above step 1 and step 2 again. If you do not see a physical copy in your favorite bookstore please act appalled, then demand to see a manager, then tell that manager you want to speak to their regional director, then tell them to get off their lazy ass and order a few hundred copies of "Wrecklessly Absurd". That way you are a hero to your community.

And that kids, is how I met your mother.

Contents of the Table

FOREWORD

Welcome back. I hope you're as happy and content in your life as can be. I hope you find some of your inner happiness while reading through my next set of crazy circumstances.

For those of you just picking up this book I will simply say, welcome. It is not imperative that you read the first book in this trilogy, "The Strange Paths We All Follow", but you will find some comments throughout this book that echo back to specific moments in that book. These stories can definitely be enjoyed as a standalone experience.

I am very glad to have each and every one of you back for the next installment of my trilogy. I would also sincerely like to thank all of you that shared in my first book. The feedback and love you showed me was not lost upon my life's path.

Since we last saw each other, my life has taken many interesting turns. I never knew that becoming an author was going to make such a difference in my life. If you got anything out of my last exposé hopefully it was that I have led a very lucky and blessed life. I also have no problem sharing my personal crazy stories in hopes that it would make some sort of difference in the reader's life. I can happily share that I indeed got that feedback from people across the entire globe. Yes. Entire globe. From Mumbai, India to Ballarat, Australia to Antarctica my first book was reviewed and read by complete strangers. I cannot even tell you what that feeling is like. Blessed indeed.

I wrote the last book for my two little monsters and dedicated it to them. You see, I have always had a life goal to write and publish something. I was not sure how that was going to happen but as I started writing a book that was dedicated out of love, things just worked out. It is weird how things work out when you do something from your heart.

This book will continue what the first started. Some stories from my life infused with a couple of guest authors that you may have read before. Yet this book is different. The last book was a collection of all the crazy stories in my life. I tried to not only make sense of the absurd, but also to hopefully give my kids, and you, an alternate perspective on life.

This book here? This one is dedicated to you. My fans, friends, and family that have all helped in their own way to make up the compilation of stories you are about to read. Thank you all for what you have given me. It is invaluable. This book is NOT perfect. Neither is life. Imperfections are what make all of us unique. So please forgive an error, or two, or three, in the upcoming pages.

I hope that each of you can find your own funny bone. Or at least I hope this book helps bring it back if in case it has gotten muddled in the noise that surrounds you every day. This is meant to be a catalyst to spark your funny memories that are stored in the recesses of your brain.

Since the last book was a look into the dangers and craziness of our collective lives, this book looks to celebrate everything life throws our way. It's an ode to the yesterday that you sometimes forget or let fade in the background. The format will be just as ADHD as myself and as my last book. I wanted to make my own style. These three books are not an autobiography or a memoir as those both follow specific rules. This is my collection of my memories.

So please turn off your brain to outside influences, put any judgement in the backseat, and simply read what comes next with reckless abandon and a very light soul. Put your worries on the backburner and take my hand while I guide you through many chapters of my life. It is my sole intention to entertain you.

#Cheers

IT'S A BIG WORLD AFTER ALL

his chapter is special. One, this chapter officially kicks off book two of this trilogy. It also sets up what book three is all about: the differences in perspectives of how people view the world and each other even though they may be recollecting the exact same event.

Also, my favorite guest author is the co-writer for this chapter as she will be on every single chapter in the final book. More on that later.

This story takes place in the very early part of our marriage. In fact, I think we were right at one full year of marriage. And we were already moving on. We had our fill of Twin Falls, Idaho. It was a great little town with all its 30,000 people. It served its purpose and now I was being re-cruited by a company in California. The land of surf, movie stars, and my buddy George. It was time for our love to bloom in a new locale.

As most newlyweds usually are, especially fresh out of college, we were flat broke. Not terrible mind you, but we were on a tight budget. That budget did not include professional drivers hauling the contents of our small apartment 600 miles from Twin Falls to Sacramento. Oh, did I mention surf, movie stars, and my buddy George? Yeah, those were in different parts of Cali, many hours south and west of Sacramento. We had Tahoe, Napa, and the Bay Area. Okay tradeoffs for not having the perfect weather and beaches of SoCal. Since we both grew up in states where you drive to go anywhere, driving the 10 hours was doable. But we needed to get a U-Haul with a trailer to haul our second car. A very inexpensive alternative to using a professional moving company.

When we picked up the truck and trailer the day before our departure, we encountered a small, well large, complication. The company did not have the U-Haul we had reserved, wreck or something. So instead of the 17-foot truck that we had rented, they only had a 26-foot in stock. No price differences. Great. The 10-foot trailer for our second car was there though. So, one day and 36 feet later we were slowly pulling away from our old lives at the Thomas Apartments. We were on our way to California.

The drive was mostly uninteresting. I remember we were stopped entering California for an agricultural check. That was about it. I am sure my better half might recount something else but that is my memory of it. Stupid truck had a regulator, so the max speed I could drive was right at 65. The trip took a couple of extra hours.

Fortunately for us, we were a good duo. The roads were wide open and the navigation of the 36 feet of metal I was in was easy. Remember, no electronics back then. My wife, Ava, had a CD player since she was driving my car, and I had 12 hours of in and out radio stations. No iPods, no cell phones. Just hope and your own two eyes to figure out your surroundings. Which ended up being our downfall in this little story.

We finally arrived in Sacramento. In full on rush hour. We both knew the address, and both knew where it was on the MapQuest we printed out. We both had only been to Sacramento once. That was when the company I was now going to work for flew us both from Twin Falls to Sacramento. It was for a quick meeting and last interview for the position I was about to start. We saw the area where we would eventually be moving to. We saw it all in a couple hours, at night. That was not nearly enough time for us to prepare for California's notorious traffic from hell.

Ava did a great job staying with me, especially since I could not move out of the lane I was in. A little too much room was needed for that. She was able to weave and bob around the traffic to get behind the truck. After a good hour in that shit, we finally came up on our exit. Luckily, I was one lane over and after many honks I was able to move over to the exit lane.

Now began our second round of hell. Sunrise Fucking Boulevard. This historic byway spans from the top part of Sacramento, in Roseville, all the way down close to Folsom, near the southeast end of Sacramento. Lucky for us, where we came in, we were a mere 15 miles to our new apartment, which was just off Sunrise Boulevard in Citrus Heights. Should have been easy even in bumper to bumper traffic. But remember, no smart phones. Just a crappy printed draft of maps with directions kind of showing me the way.

I should also point out that my wife, bless her soul, grew up in Wyoming, Iowa, Montana, and most recently the rurals of Twin Falls, Idaho. That was her formative traffic experience years. I at least had the pleasure of driving around to major metropolises like Spokane and Boise. This was her first foray into driving on major highway arteries and experiencing traffic flow. Especially at rush hour.

As I exited, I looked back. Beyond my 36-foot entourage I was pulling, I could see Ava was about six or seven cars behind. But I did see that she was at least on the same exit as me. The good news, and bad news, was we both exited Sunrise Boulevard. Let me make something clear for the Sacramentans: I know it's technically Douglas Boulevard down to Sunrise Avenue which then turns into Sunrise Boulevard. To this day, for Ava and me, it will always be referred to as Sunrise Fucking Boulevard.

As I pulled off, I realized the traffic was going to get way worse. This must have been a major artery for not only where people lived, but also for people who were trying to avoid the I-80 which was already grid-locked. We would come to learn the longer we lived in Sactown how true this was. It was when we turned onto what should have been our final stretch of the Boulevard that hell went straight into the handbasket.

As I came within a mere five miles from our exit to our about to be brand new condo, that mind you, we rented out of the back of a rental magazine (remember, no real internet kiddos), it was then that I realized my wife was no longer in sight. She didn't know any better, and with those beautiful spud license plates, she didn't stand a chance. She was cut into and pushed out of lanes she didn't even know existed. She was about twenty cars back now. I had all but lost sight of the little black Acura she was driving.

I became so worried about where she was at that I totally blanked out where I was at and what apartment complex name I was looking for. I was also concentrating on the stop and go traffic that I was up against. I could not move lanes if I wanted to. My 36 feet of obtrusive metal was not making the locals happy. I was stuck in the left lane whether I wanted to be or not. I had no clue where my wife was.

As I cruised my way past our new home's exit, I was still more con-centrated on Ava coming into view. Surely, she could see the SS Min-now Twin Falls in her view? I was in the extra-large Ryder truck and the

26-foot trailer towing the white whale. Everyone else could see me and was honking at my yokel ass. It took me about an extra ten miles to real-ize I had missed my turn. At this time, I had no choice, wife be damned.

I made the first left I could. Which, in my opinion, was the worst met-aphorical and physical left I have ever taken in my entire life. As I pulled into the quaint apartment complex roundabout, I had a quick choice to make. I could only go left or right. Once again, I took the wrong left.

As I started to head down the rows of parked cars, I realized I was coming to a dead end. There was nowhere to really turn around. I knew I couldn't go straight, as there was nowhere to turn this beast I was driving around. I saw a wide enough turn to my left again, and hoped it led back to the front of the complex to leave and hope to catch my wife some-where in the traffic mess. How wrong I was.

I got the corner navigated well enough. I cut the trailer a little close but didn't think much of it as I was now headed back to the front. Ex-cept, I wasn't. I realized right after I turned in, I had gone straight into a dead-end dumpster area. There was nowhere to go straight ahead of me. Also, there was no place to turn this Titanic ship around. I was smashed into this area like a trapped sardine with only one way to go. Backwards. Also, I was the only one around. It was in the early evening rush, and these condos looked deserted. I still had no clue where my wife was. There was little to no chance in hell she saw me turn into the apartment complex.

I tried for what seemed like an hour to slowly back this monster up, by myself, with simply just the backup mirrors. I was so wedged into this strip of road that I was doing nothing but making it worse. I had condos to my left, only about 10 feet away, my back trailer already on top of their concrete patios. To the right I had the complex gates. Each time I was backing up I was way too close to hitting everything. It was not as easy as putting it in reverse and backing up. This fucking car trailer was not working with my wheel motions in the 36-foot U-Haul truck.

After what seemed like another hour, I finally was greeted by this nice, very old lady. Seems she was one of the few at her house at that time and was joyfully watching me in my predicament. She figured it was about time to try to help a fellow citizen out. Plus, she wanted her condo to stay intact and not become part of my car trailer.

This was about to become even more comical. Here was this 4'2", 85-year-old lady trying to stand near the back and give me wheel turn instructions. Bless her heart to this day. Sadly, it was, how does the saying go? The blind leading the blind. At least she tried.

After about thirty minutes of this Seinfeld moment, the rest of the apartment complex started humming back to life. They also realized this huge moving truck was in their backyard. So sure enough, person by person, they came out to gawk at the dumbass who drove his house into their backyard walking path. The only shining light in this debacle was that I had about six other eyeballs now helping me back this monster out. Sadly, I had no choice but to back straight up into their rapidly filling parking spaces, causing some well understood frustration at not being able to get by me.

It took a solid hour to get out of this pinhole. When I finally was faced back towards the exit to Sunrise Fucking Boulevard, I realized I had been missing from my wife for about two hours, in a town we had never been to when we were driving. I assumed the worse. While I was frustrated beyond my boiling point, I now had to figure out how to find my wife. Again, no cell phone, no beeper. Nada. Just two eyeballs and 36 feet of solid metal fun underneath my ass.

As I pulled back out of the apartment complex and I was on Sunrise Fucking Boulevard again. As I was edging my rental truck's nose into the new traffic jam, I noticed what looked like my car, the one my wife was driving, across the street but going the other way. When I saw Ava's face there was a sort of relief yet still anger on both of our faces. The relief was that she did not get lost in this foreign city, but also that at that moment in time, even being lost from each other, we happened to connect.

I frantically pointed to her to follow me back to the apartment complex. The nice people that directed me out of their backyard told me where I needed to go. We needed to go sign paperwork to get our place. The new place was just about a half mile down Sunrise Fucking Boulevard. Mind you, I had not had contact with Ava for a couple of hours at this point. All I knew is that I had about fifteen minutes to get us to the office to sign our contract and get the keys. Otherwise we would not be able to see them until the next day.

As I was pulling into our new apartment complex, I realized I had about two minutes to spare to catch the office managers and get settled in to our new California life. Little did I know, there was another side to this story. Because every story has different perspectives. Always. But let me let Ava tell you her side.

*

One year. We spent one year in Twin Falls, Idaho and that was enough. Or so I decided as I sat next to the microfiche reader in the community college library, pouring through actual want ads in local newspapers. I was still lacking any semblance of a career path, so I focused on Chance. There had to be something he could do with all the fancy financial planning he was doing at Norwest Financial (former finance company of the then esteemed Wells Fargo Bank) located next to the Little Caesars Pizza. I mean, he had a whole year's experience of financing treadmills and couches at 32 percent and, I believed, was ready for something great.

"Growing auto finance company seeks qualified candidate for outside sales. Competitive salary with bonuses." No company name and no phone number. Just a P.O. Box with a California address. I immediately crafted an outstanding cover letter and resume for a job that, even today, I admit I do not fully understand. I dropped it in the mailbox and told Chance over dinner at Applebee's. He looked at me and said, "Cool."

The following week Chance received a call from someone who wanted to fly, yes fly, both Chance and I to California for an interview. What?!?!?! That only happened to real grownups. We had officially arrived.

We spent a fabulous weekend in the sophisticated city of Sacramento being wined and dined. We were so important that they even drove us to Reno, Nevada for a night at the Peppermill Casino, including the buffet. It was legit.

A few days later, I brought Chance a Jamba Juice at work (don't be jealous) and he handed me a sticky note that said, "I got the job." Goodbye Thomas apartments and Republican red Idaho and hello California!

We were headed to the west coast - no actual relocation package - but we were moving on up. We did the obvious grown-up thing and immediately called our parents to ask for money for our big move. With parental funding, we rented the largest U-Haul truck available and a trailer for our Mercury Topaz. On move-out day, we carried everything from our second story apartment into the truck, dropped the key in the manager's mailbox (there was no need to actually tell anyone we were moving out), and drove out of town to a new life.

There were two solid days of driving through the desolate lands of Idaho and Nevada. My view was the back of the U-Haul truck never going a mile over 65 mph thanks to the safety of the speed regulator. Eventually, the Sierra Nevada

Mountains came into view along with the glorious 'Welcome to California' sign. There was a checkpoint for illegal produce. My heart stopped. I had a mini panic attack as I watched the border official walk up to Chance's window. I forgot to mention that in the trunk of the Topaz on top of the trailer was a microwave. Inside the microwave was a single sunflower plant that Chance had been so lovingly growing for the last four months. Even though he knew he could not bring plants into California, he decided he was above that law. No need to worry, though. Chance handed the man an apple core and he waved us through with good wishes for our new beginning in the Golden State.

Everything was going to be ok. We just had to make it to the gated community of Sunrise Commons by 5:00 PM to claim our key for the fabulous apartment we had rented sight unseen from a For Rent magazine. The pictures had been in black and white, but the price was right - $695.00 per month. This was $200.00 more than we had been paying in Idaho, but there was a clubhouse and a pool. And, Chance would be making $36,000.

Due to our brilliant timing, we hit Sacramento traffic at exactly 3:30 on a Friday afternoon. We were way out of our element. I was going into full panic mode - traffic, bridges, multi-lane highways, and people. We of course had no cell phones. But I knew my job was to go slow and lead the way to Sunrise Commons. I exited the highway and headed down Sunrise Boulevard. Occasionally I would glance in my rearview mirror to make sure the Ryder truck was behind me. I was doing ok, until I was not.

At about 4:00, I did my glance back and there was no yellow truck. My heart stopped and then began to race. WHERE THE FUCK WAS HE???!!! How had he possibly disappeared on this ridiculous boulevard with bumper-to-bumper traffic moving at a snail's pace?

I spent the next 58 minutes driving up and down Sunrise Boulevard vacillating between panic, anger, and utter desperation. I COULD NOT FIND

THAT TRUCK. It was like 100 degrees, I had to go to the bathroom badly, and everyone around me was crazy. Why did we ever want to live here? I was absolutely convinced that Chance had decided he did not want to do this, had gotten back on the highway, and was heading back. I was going to be a divorcee with no job, no money, and an apartment I could not pay for. I was so furious while at the same time wanting to see him with my whole heart.

I could not find Chance, but if I didn't get to Sunrise Commons by 5:00 I wouldn't be able to get the keys until Monday morning. I would be living in my car for two days. I made the decision to forgo the search for the missing yellow truck and go get the keys. And then, like it was dropped from the sky, next to me was the yellow Ryder truck. Relief flooded over me and I led Chance into the gated community at 4:59. I didn't know where he'd been or what he'd been doing for an hour, but when they handed us our keys, I knew that if we had survived Sunrise Fucking Boulevard, we would be just fine in California.

*

Different perspectives complete a story. I think there is so much of that in life that we all have stepped away from remembering. So many people are sure their perspective is the only perspective they may miss the rest of the story. I am all for being right and standing up for what you believe in. I just hope that something to take away from this is that there is always more to the story. It might feel good, it might make you upset, but there is also another perspective that has so many different attributes; some you might not have even imagined or stereotypes you didn't realize you had. Sometimes it makes sense to take a deep breath, survey the scene around you, clear your mind of the problem at hand, and sit back and try your hardest to see if you can figure out what that other perspective is.

This is the first, but not the last time I will test that resolve throughout the rest of this funny ride you take in the rest of this book. Now turn off your judgments and open your sense of morality and read the rest of this with an open mind.

Fake Jube Days

I absolutely loved our life when we moved back to Colorado. Northern California was awesome, and I became much more in tune with myself and my wife, but Colorado is where my heart and soul belong.

We were lucky enough that not only did we get to spend time with my family back in Montana, but we also got the added benefit of being able to hang out with my wife's family in northern and southern Wyoming. Both fantastic, exotic lands that we called home and roamed around in freely. We never took it for granted. It felt right, but we knew the luck we had being around this beautiful land and all that encompasses it.

One of those beautiful gems we got to explore was the town of Laramie. A small college town bustling with the joy of Wyoming's only football team (Go Cowboys!) A whole other world in the wild, wild west.

Laramie had quite a few things to celebrate. Author Chip Rawlins was from there, so was Olympic athlete Jessica Cross. Teenage Bottlerocket, an up and coming punk band, also hails from this fair city.

Plus, my wife's mother and father fell in love and started their family there. Sadly, the city is also known for the murder of Matthew Shepard. That's a story for you to look up.

One of their larger festivities was Jubilee Days, which in 2018 marked their 78th year of existence. It started in 1940 to celebrate Wyoming Statehood Day. It is a weeklong celebration of the Old West and those activities that honor the lives of those who came before as well as current leaders and trendsetters of Wyoming. It begins with a kids' horse show and ends with the PRCA Rodeo. A lot of people descend on this sleepy town for a good time and jubilation.

Laramie is also a college party town, no different than where I grew up. A ton of directionless youth with dreams, ambitions, and a sense of exploration. Funny thing is, I never lost the sense to explore. For good or for bad. This particular story involves some of my favorite travel partners, George and Frank.

As it came about, we were invited to Laramie by my wife's family. They were all coming to town and we would celebrate a fun family weekend. Her family already had house guests, so when we asked if there was extra room it was met with an emphatic, "Bring them!". Frank and George really had no choice, they had come to Denver to visit and this opportunity came up. My wife wanted to go so they were not about to say no. It would be a new adventure for them, and it would be a place that they never visited. It was a win-win situation.

We made our three-hour ride from south Denver in easy fashion. We had stayed up late the night prior with the usual recanting of the stories you have read so far and ones that may never see the light of day in any of my books. It was nothing new to have Ava driving the three assholes to her next embarrassment. Do not feel too bad for her. She would tell you herself that she has a special place in her heart for all my friends. Plus, guaranteed fun. Guaranteed laughs.

We finally reached my brother-in-law's place and it was already full to the brim. It was a huge home, but the entire family was there. My wife's parents, my wife's sister and her current husband, Ronnie, and then George and Frank whom the family already knew and sort of accepted.

We immediately began exploring downtown Laramie and looking for the hustle and bustle that surely came with Jubilee Days. It was the largest celebration next to Homecoming in this little windy town. The stars aligned and my wife's best friend and maid of honor in our wedding was in town. She and her new hubby were meeting up with some of their friends.

As we drove down to the main eatery, we were surprised to see very little advertising for the upcoming town holiday. A couple of things mentioned the day and some banners with the logo but not much at all. Which was odd as the big parade would be near this route. No big deal. We rolled into the restaurant and met up with Suzy and her husband. My wife and Suzy were catching up when I asked Suzy if they were also in town for Jubilee Days. Her blank stare pretty much summed up everything. What she said next confirmed it: we were a week off. Jubilee Days started next week. We had been hoodwinked by my wife's little brother. He had told us it was Jubilee weekend.

Funny enough it was a "whatever" from this point on. It wasn't going to stop our weekend. We were still hanging out with great people; we would make the best of it. Of course, Frank and George, being lifelong buddies and true friends for over thirty years, had to point out the fact that I dragged them up to "Fake Jube Days". It would live up to its own namesake.

We all ended up laughing it off and enjoying ourselves through the rest of the day. Great dinner with the in-laws and friends and then a relaxing night out with Suzy and her old man. We hit a nice dance club that night and shook and jimmied our excess energy out. All and all, incident free. The first day of two nights in Laramie for Fake Jube Days was already successful!

Day 2 began with an uneventful morning. A couple laughs at George's dancing skills the prior night. An alarming outpour for why Frank must keep taking off his shirt in the bar near the end of the night. Some storytelling of Jubilee Days past. Again, great start to the day. This is where the train left the tracks.

Ava woke up with a headache. Migraines are the mother of a merciless god. They have always been debilitating for her. My mother-in-law and her youngest son decided to go on a day long hike with some of the kids. The older brother-in-law and my father-in-law decide to take the dinghy out to the local pond to do some fishing. My sister-in-law and her hubby had been deciding what to do. As it turned out, he ended up open as she wanted to go visit a few of her old college buddies that still lived in Laramie. That left Ronnie to accept whatever Frank, George, and I decided to do. We decided quick that we were going to continue in Jubilee fashion. I knew the local bar would be a great kick off for the real Jubilee Days was just a stone's throw away from my brother-in-law's. So, off the four of us went, like the Goonies looking for that damn ship.

Our ship was found very quickly. Her name? Minglers. One of the oddest bars in America.

We walked in expecting the place was going to be jam packed like on a St. Patrick's Day, but there were three people in the entire bar. Fake Jube Days was upon us. Of course, none of that mattered. Christ's sake, it was only 11am. The local drunks don't even show up until noon at this place. No big deal. What this bar offered was exactly what we wanted to do on this random Saturday afternoon. We spotted the twenty open pool tables in the back, grabbed a couple of pitchers, and started our bar Olympics.

This place had it all; pool tables, darts, shuffleboard, beer pong, Golden Tee, Big Buck Hunter, and a few other things. The four of us had about four or five hours until we were needed for anything important, so we were going to imbibe and let loose a little extra energy from the night before. And we did.

Let me tell you something about Wyoming. It is a beautiful state full of a diverse cast of characters as well as the rugged landscapes that engulf it. It also might just be the cheapest state to drink. Hell, the night before, we were all out and buying rounds for 10 or more of us. In Vegas, that one round would be upwards of $150. Just for one fucking round. Granted you get Kim Kardashian in your face or DJ Boyer Krunk throwing down some sweet tunes to offset the small loan you just paid to get your friends drunk. Wyoming? Not so much. More on that important part later.

There were a few more people who trickled in, but we didn't care. The four of us were placing bets, talking shit, and going through beer faster than a fat kid goes through cake. FYI, that is not a knock on fat kids. Three out of four of us were fat and having a fucking blast.

It was approaching two o'clock and Ronnie was starting to regret his decision. Plus, he was anxious to return to his wife and stay out of his usual doghouse. He had a blast with us, but he wanted to bow out. We told him to just leave us 50 bucks and that should cover his three hours of drinking plus bar games. He gladly paid and sauntered out of the joint with a small buzz. He would later realize what a good decision he had made that day.

George, Frank, and me? We were good. We were having a fucking blast. We were all even Steven and slowly marching towards something glorious. Little did we know we had around three hours until anyone would legally declare us missing. We started ordering 32-ounce Red Bull Vodkas. At the time we thought it was a great idea. Did I mention it was a glorious day? Until the end?

So along we went. More bets, more drinks. We thought that Fake Jube Days should become a yearly tradition. Then, just like that, it was time to leave. My wife sent me a text for an exact time and place the three of us needed to be. I let my buddies know. They slammed down their drinks and were ready for the next party.

The three of us stumbled up to the bar to pay our inevitable tab. It was coming. We knew it was going to be big. We have all been out together in multiple cities, and with multiple people comes huge eating and drinking bills. This was almost seven hours of unjudged and unadulterated binge drinking. Something NO ONE should ever do, to be fair. We completely expected a bill of around a grand with what we drank as well as what Ronnie had before he left us. Ronnie generally drank a third of his weight alone. Thank god he gave us fifty bucks to cover his four hours. Always super helpful and thoughtful, that Ronnie.

Then it happened. Our karmic positivity finally paid off. Weird it was at a place like Minglers. We got the bill. Among the two pages of required drink orders was a number. A number unlike one we have ever seen or experienced. A number so low that it must be a sign.

Our bill, for almost seven hours of drinking heavily, buying some newfound friends drinks, and the hours of pool, shuffleboard, and other video games we played and paid for. That bill? $99.00. Yep. $99.00. Did I mention that everyone living in or visiting the United States should put Wyoming on their must-see list? For many, many reasons. Such a lovely place.

We stumbled gleefully out into the high elevation sun which immediately pierced our indoor, vampire sun tans. With the small bar stock that was coursing through our bodies at that moment, we vaguely realized we had a few more blocks to my brother-in-law's but also, we needed to bring back some beers for the rest of the family. We had agreed to pick that up on the way home from our afternoon vacation.

We bumbled our way through the Albertsons grocery store across from Minglers. We somehow managed to grab all the stuff that my wife's family had asked for. Mind you that ask was now about 45 minutes ago. George even had a hankering for some nostalgia and decided he was going to rope the wind with some fresh chewing tobacco. Whatever. His choice. We were finally out of the store and headed to meet the long-lost family.

When we rounded the back of the grocery store, there was a small two-lane road we had to navigate to get to the turn where my brother-in-law's place was. As we made that turn, George started to make the most recognizable, especially to us, gut wrenching sound. The chaw habit did not quite kick back in. Not like riding a bike. The past six hours of booze was coming up. At least he made it to the corner of the building before emptying the contents of his poor abused body. Frank and I had seen this so many times it didn't even phase us. As we stopped to let George pay his respects to Albertsons, we heard a distinct yell from behind us.

Two girls drove by us in a small VW Beetle. The one on the right leaned out and yelled something our drunk, old minds couldn't comprehend.

We instinctively yelled and waved back. Lo and behold, they actually turned around. Why did that shit not happen in high school? Now that I think about it, it could have possibly been the three cases of beer they saw us lugging around. I digress. They slowed down next to Frank and me. George had slightly recovered and noticed we were talking to someone, so he slowly sauntered over to us with his chest puffed out like a Puffin bird.

The ladies were just being nice. They wanted to know if we needed a ride, especially with the six cases of beer we were toting around with us. We looked old and clumsy, so these nice citizens were just doing their civic duty. Two big guys and a skinny guy. We thought we would fit fine in the back of the small Beetle. So off we went. Frank was the first clown who tried to fit in the clown car. This would shave off a total of ten minutes of walking time so we would be somewhat early for the request that was made of us, which was simply get home for dinner and bring beer.

That exact point is where I can pinpoint one of the most bizarre, fucked up scenes that has ever unfolded in my life.

I looked over my shoulder and there was a cop car about 20 feet away. It pulled right in front of the girls Beetle. He had his lights on and exited his car holding up the universal hand signal for, "Stop or I'll shoot." We all froze. Except George. His puke fest was over, and he was still stumbling down the loading bay of the supermarket.

The cop looked toward big Frank still stuck halfway in the Beetle and then started barking orders. "What the hell are you idiots doing? You sir, get out of the backseat of the car or I will taser your ass!" Both George and I stop dead in our tracks. "I saw you guys from the start. I saw you go in and buy a shit ton of beer, I saw you stumble around the corner, and then saw your buddy back there puke all over the side of the building! Now what the hell are you doing with these young ladies!?" By this time Frank had squeezed back out of the clown car.

"Sir, we were just trying to get back to my buddy's family's house a few blocks away," he somehow slurred.

The drunken gibberish that came out of Frank's mouth, or maybe his erratic hand gestures for indication purposes, spooked the cop.

"Get your hands on top of the car, turn around, and spread 'em! You too pukey boy!" he growled.

We all dropped the cases of beer we were escorting back to my in-laws and did as requested. The cop was leveling his Taser gun directly towards us.

He proceeded to come up and ask the girls what the hell they were thinking. They said they saw us, and we looked like we needed some help, so they figured they would stop and help like a good Samaritan. They said they always liked to help the elderly when they could. Ouch.

He then proceeded to round up our licenses. He was calling in our info to dispatch when I happened to turn my head and see the worst sight possible. Right down the street, the way we would have been walking, was a parked SUV with its lights on. It was my SUV, with my wife, her brothers, her sister and sister's husband. Watching this all unfold. Well, fuck.

You see we apparently were not as fast as we thought we were going to be. It turned out my wife thought it would be nice to come pick us up with the family on the way to a different friend's house for a BBQ. Just as they turned the corner, they happened to see a cop car blaze past them. Then they pulled over to watch that cop stop a little Volkswagen Beetle a block and a half in front of where they pulled over. Then my wife and in-laws proceeded to watch myself and my two buddies get ordered into detention positions from the cop that just passed them.

I will have to have her tell you her side of the story sometime. I'm sure it was as entertaining but more infuriating coming from a different perspective.

The police officer came back to us. "OK you morons. You are cleared to leave. Both party's stories jive. Next time make sure to just walk the entire way home. Maybe not get into a car of teenagers with a boat load of alcohol?" Oh shit. We never got a good glance at the ladies as they simply drove by. Plus, we were near the college, so we just assumed they were college aged kids heading over to campus. Now we understood why the cop came in blazing. Luckily there was no Chris Hansen from Dateline NBC riding with that cop.

We thanked everyone involved. The girls sped away. The cop drove past us, disappointingly shaking his head towards the three of us. Then we sulked over to my wife. She did not even move a bit. They sat and watched the entire situation unfold. My wife was not looking too thrilled. My brother in law, who had left us just a few hours prior, was laughing like a madman. Mainly because it was finally someone else in the glare of the shitstorm, as 90% of the time it was usually him caught up in that storm. Ronnie had stolen a lot of bikes in his lifetime.

"What the hell??!!" Ava said in a firm, but louder than usual tone.

Before I could say a thing, good old George and Frank decided to take over. "Ava, this was not our fault. Well, maybe a little. But all we were trying to do is make it home as directed and get you guys some beer as a nice gesture for having us as guests. We also were simply being lazy and accepted a ride from some nice girls." George said in a drunken slur. My wife also did not seem amused by that answer either.

"Look, I know that all looked bad, but here is the deal. We got the beer, we were intentionally heading back to the house, and the cop did not give us a ticket. That's the bottom line," I stoically tried to say.

My wife gave it thought, realized her drunk audience and exactly who they were and simply said, "Well, I guess that's why I still love you. At least you idiots did the right thing and did not drive anywhere in your drunken state." That was the end of what could have been a very bad blow up. That was all that ever needed to be said.

We stopped going to Fake Jube Days after that trip. Also, come to think of it, I have not been asked to bring my buddies back to Ava's family events. Huh.

WITH FRIENDS LIKE US

Vegas. Ahhhhhhh Vegas. The best worst city in the world. There is something poetic about the neon lights interacting with the tragic hooker walking down the boulevard with her dignity slowly trailing behind her. There is so much beauty and danger in so few square miles.

I had been to Vegas multiple times prior to this trip I am about to describe. These trips always ended the same. A large dent in my bank account and a hangover that was going to last for the next fucking week. But the stories. Ohhhhh the stories. Always grand and mostly unmentionable. Not this one.

It was already being billed as the best boys' trip that our group had assembled yet. Most of the main crew was there. Chris, Frank, Wookie, and George were all in attendance and in usual tip top form. Chris had invited some of his new buddies from Phoenix, so we had about twelve guys total for this trip. We were young and stupid. You never roll to Vegas with more than four guys in the same group. I can't even recall what the occasion was for. A birthday maybe? I know for sure it was not one of Chris's umpteenth bachelor parties. Seriously, that dude needs to stop getting married.

As usual I had come in a night earlier than the agreed upon arrival date. I always do that. I think I like the silence before the obnoxious, but still with the effects of the trip around me. As it so happened, George and Chris were able to join me. Typical shit show night in Vegas.

We at least made the correct choice on our choice of accommodations. Generally, we just stayed at the cheapest hotel on the strip. We all agreed that it was dumb to waste money on a room when we would be using it to sleep, shower, and shave. Like I said, we were stupid back then. I should also point out that this was older Vegas. That era did not have all the cool pools nor the parties that accompanied them. We happened to find one of those early pool parties on this trip. We were all staying at The Hard Rock hotel, known for their Rehab parties at their brand-new pools. We finally picked a place that had more to offer than just a bed and a shower.

We got up after our first night and headed straight to the pool party. The rest of the crew would all be coming in at random times throughout the day and later that night. The important part to this story is the fact our group all ended up on the same floor in our hotel. We all would be neighbors for the next three days. Which was convenient for so many different reasons.

By that evening we had assembled the entire Avengers team. It was a classic case of a bunch of fucktards from every possible background you could think of. A huge group of likeminded gentlemen that could throw down; a perfect storm if I ever saw one. But this chapter is not about that.

One of Chris's new buddies, that we were just meeting, was kind of a shy kid. He really did not have any reason to be, and he wasn't going to get a chance to be. We are a trial by fire type of group. We walk you off the plank the first time you meet us, but at least we jump in right after we throw you off. Metaphorically speaking.

His name was Rick. Rick the pool boy. Well, not really. He worked for a pool company in the day but was an aspiring wakeboard male model in the night. Super cool dude. Reminder though, the majority of our group was meeting him for the very first time.

As you may have previously read, and will continue to read, I have a penance for laughter. It rules my life, and quite frankly it should rule yours as well. I have never met a happy person who was sad. That makes no sense, but I know what I mean. The prior night to everyone coming in Chris and I got up to our old third grade pranks. We were able to mess with George's room. Nothing terrible. We just made his sheets half of his bed. Short sheeted as the prank was called. Innocent and stupid but so entertaining for us. So much so we decided we were going to pull off some more pranks on Chris's new party members.

When the Phoenicians arrived, it was late enough to hit up a group dinner. We had booked some stupid expensive sushi restaurant that George raved about. George would of course end up buying the group dinner. His choice as he loved to be the big shot in front of new people, kind of his thing. No one complained when the $1,000 bill came, and George swooped it up.

It was during that dinner that I would excuse myself, and Chris would too, and we would run up to the block of rooms to achieve our third-grade inner child needs. Chris had acquired Rick's room key. He was rooming with another new member, Dizzle. Both of whom I had just met but Chris had now known for a few years. He assured me that these were the right two to play this prank on.

Again, it was all innocent. We turned over all the furniture in their room. Did some short sheets for both of their beds. We needed more though. Then we remembered we saw some just emptied room service trays next door. Kind of gross, but we put the half-eaten sandwiches on their beds. Not in their beds, we are not animals! The kicker was the used saran wrap from that eaten food. I told Chris that I had the best idea ever. I would use that Saran Wrap the top of the toilet bowl and then close the lid. The poor sap who took a pee would unfortunately have to clean up their excrement as it would bounce off the unseen Saran Wrap and end up all over the bathroom floor. Jesus did that silly prank pay off in ways that we could not have imagined.

Chris and I were gone long enough for the group to ask if we were fucking each other in the bathroom. We assured them that our anal virginity was still intact and that we just got caught up chatting. I told them I was consulting Chris about a new girl he just started dating and wanted to know if he should marry her. Sadly, everyone in the group understood that conversion as they all had that same type of conversation with Chris over the years. The group went on to shots and Chris and I chuckled to ourselves thinking of poor Dizzle or Rick getting back to their room that night.

The rest of the night went about as normal as can be when a large group of guys go to Vegas. We tried multiple clubs only to get kicked out, or the line was way too long, and our patience was at zero. As it turned out, we never needed to leave the Hard Rock. It had everything we would need. We ended up at the afterhours club there, then back at the tables to gamble away our future retirement funds.

We still had the entire group intact, which is saying a lot as it was very close to morning and we had been going hard all day. Wookie was close to done. He was stumbling around with his usual 1000-yard stare that he always had right before blackout mode. No shit, he sat behind about five of us playing blackjack and passed out. Not even 5 minutes later there was some random chick sucking face with him. Who the fuck gets a hook up while dead drunk passed out? This chapter is not about that.

The gambling floor was packed. The weird thing was that there was an unusual amount of stunningly beautiful woman around. I mean, it was easily a sixty-forty split in favor of girls to guys which was a little odd. What was even more weird was that some of those ladies were talking with much of our group. Not for naught, we have some decent looking and very charismatic guys, but we were 7's and 8's and these ladies were legit 9's and 10's. Being one of the only married guys in the group I was lucky to adopt a drunken Wookie and got to watch the other guys from confines of the sideline.

Male model Rick, in all his 5-foot 1-inch stature, had somehow gotten the attention of one of the hottest girls in the pack. She was even laughing at whatever he was telling her. Then a kiss. Holy crap, Rick was here on his first night and he was going to have the story of a lifetime in a group of guys that are all used to being the subject of that said story. Sure enough, Rick wished us all a good night and went sauntering off with his brand-new friend. We had only just met the little surfer dude and already he was making a five-star impression on all of us.

Did I mention that we were all stupid? I don't want anyone to take this out of context. I am blessed to have the friends I do, and the new ones I continuously meet. My friends run businesses, fly planes, make bike gang videos, sell used telecom wiring, and so on. When I say we are all stupid, I mean it in the best way. You see, as we all sort of got to talking to all these ladies, there was literally a collective "click" of the light bulb all at once. Or maybe it was that Frank was told a price if he would like to take the girl he was flirting with upstairs. Ohhhhhh . . .

Yup. These ladies didn't give two fucks about our dumb ass stories or our jokes. Nope. They cared about our bank accounts. These were ladies of opportunity. Some old fables describe them as ladies of the night. Hookers. Did I mention we were stupid?

Not a big deal. These encounters happen in life. One of Chris's buddies negotiated a price and took his new date upstairs. For the most part though, my buddies are not that desperate for a night cap as to part with their hard-earned money for that pleasure. To each to their own. I am not passing judgement on either side of that coin.

This chapter is all about that next day. The next afternoon to be exact. Because as we all left the opportunistic ladies at the bar and went back to our rooms to get a little sleep, we didn't realize the sun was starting to come up. We wouldn't wake up until noon the next day to get the next party started.

The very last person to meet up at the pool the next day was Rick. We almost forgot about him and his departure. Did he know she was a prostitute? Surely, he had to know? When he finally showed up at the pool he was visibly pissed. Uh oh. Don't even know this guy for twenty-four hours and already we have a Debbie Downer. He slid into the pool with us.

The first thing we asked him is if he knew that he had taken a paid girlfriend back to his room. He was getting more visibly upset. Then we realized he wasn't as upset as we all thought, he just had a huge red welt on the side of his face that was facing us. It was then he decided to tell us what really happened.

He did indeed figure out that he had taken a lady of repute up to his room. She told him so about a minute after crossing the threshold of his shared room. She immediately laid out the prices and services, a verbal menu if you will. It was then he was aware that his charm and spikey hair were not all that. He embarrassedly pointed out that he was not in tune that she was a street worker and that as much as he appreciated the sentiment and options, he was going to have to pass on said menu items as tempting as they were. She seemed a little annoyed but also inferred this wasn't the first time this had happened. She asked if she could use his restroom before returning to her friends' downstairs. He happily obliged and sat on the end of his bed to let her finish up and escort her back downstairs.

It was about fifteen seconds after she disappeared that he heard a scream and then some very foul words coming from his new friend. He got up to see what the issue was, and she stormed out of the re-stroom towards Rick and slapped him with her open palm. He noticed she must have been drunk because she had gotten water all up and down her beautiful dress.

He was stunned and confused. Was she now pissed about the de-clined invitation? Or was she embarrassed that she had gotten water all over herself. So many questions that she was not allowing to be answered. The only thing she yelled as she stormed out of the room was something to the effect of "I do not know what kind of sick shit you are into mother fucker! Fuck you, and your dumbass fucking friends! Fucking assholes!" Some other pleasantries could be heard coming from the hallway. She slammed the door and stormed off.

Still perplexed beyond belief at the events that just transpired, Rick walked into the bathroom. It was also about that time he noticed things were not normal in his room. Why was his chair upside down on the desk? Whose dirty food tray was on the other bed? Then it hit him like a ton of bricks. The pool of yellow around the edge of the bottom of the toilet was telling. The puddles of yellow piss that were also suspended seemingly in midair by saran wrap also told another very telling story. This stranger had just pissed all over herself and the entire area around the toilet. Our little innocent third grade joke of putting Saran Wrap around the bowl had paid off better than we could ever imagine.

Our group and the Phoenicians are not as tight as we used to be. In fact, we thought it was odd that Rick didn't invite many of us to his wedding a few years back. Who knows? Maybe he just didn't want anyone around him to know about the one time a hooker literally pissed herself in his hotel room. I guess there are probably things that some people shouldn't know. That said, I still like to randomly call Rick at any time of the day or night and wish him a very happy birthday. Just so we are clear, it's never his actual birthday. Friends never let a silly little joke get in the way of true friendship.

A boxing match is just someone trying to count to 10 but they are constantly being interrupted by a fistfight between two other people. ~ Anonymous

WHAT'S YOUR WALLET'S STORY?

The ways people interact with one another is still perplexing to me to this very day. I guess I was raised on the golden rule of treat others as you would want to be treated. The amount of daily drama people put themselves through as well as those around them baffles me. The one thing I do understand, however, is that when alcohol or drugs are introduced, that baffling behavior becomes a little more explainable. I do mean "a little".

This story involves the latter.

In my previous business life, with a previous unnamed large corporation, I oversaw business to business sales. This meant I was head of the line to speak with a multitude of different decision makers. Sometimes this included regional directors that worked for huge multi corporations themselves. You know, the type of individual that is paid a shit ton of money and doesn't necessarily deal with the "front" line rep. They go up the ladder to regionals or CEO's. High level decision makers.

I never understood that logic or chain of command. I respect every person's time and space, but I just never bought in on the fact that only one person with a specific title can only talk to this "other" type of person with a different specific title. I guess I did understand it, but I always thought "who the hell doesn't want to talk with me?" I would come to find out that the answer is a small handful of people. Guess those aren't bad odds for someone in sales. I'll take it.

In this previous company we had major brand awareness. The company had plenty of money and even more power. Everyone knew this company's commercials and everyone in my line of work knew this company's reputation. It was about half and half of whether the business clients actually liked the company, regardless of who worked there. I happened to work in a state and territory where this business wasn't really loved. They were barely tolerated. Everything I had to do to grow the territory and make some money was an absolute struggle. I had to fight, and every sale had to be a negotiation. Never any easy wins. On top of that struggle the clientele I was dealing with generally did not have the best reputation either. It was a ball busting way to make a living. Long hours, lower pay, and stress every single day.

The one huge perk to my job was that this company had ties into all major entertainment events. I had a box at multiple NFL stadiums around the US to entertain big clients. The company sponsored collegiate sports so we would get to go to bowl games and NCAA tourneys. From time to time I would get trips paid for my wife and me to take these clients to company sponsored events. It made up a tiny bit for the longer hours and stressful environment. I also was blessed with a decent monthly budget to wine and dine as I saw fit. One of the things I always tried to do was something unique that the client wouldn't already do within their organization. My intimate knowledge of music helped with picking out some exceptional concerts and my younger demographic helped with choosing interesting restaurants or bars. Getting the client out of the work environment was always key in building closer relationships and thus resulted in better sales.

It was late November and my marketing department gave me some unique tickets to take some of my business buddies to. I was given six tickets, all awesome seats, to go see the Trans-Siberian Orchestra. I vaguely knew who they were. I had heard a couple of their metal Christmas covers, but other than that knew nothing more. I would take my wife, as this was a date type of event. I had no clue on what other client couples I could possibly invite. The tickets were for a Sunday which was great as it was a guaranteed day off for my clients. It would help make my decision a little easier.

Even better was the fact my helped me mold that decision. A month prior to the concert tickets being given to me, we had agreed to a very long, oft negotiated, contract signed with a huge car dealership corporate chain. A contract that was 12 years in the making. It happened that where I lived had a large concentration of this said dealership client. It would be beneficial for me, in more ways than one.

At the very first get together with the main players within this group, I knew I had a foot in the door. I knew a ton of people within this large group from previous business dealings. The people I didn't know were the top executives. As it turned out I got to meet many of them at our first group meeting. One of the regional presidents happened to come meet me as my mutual friends within his organization had pushed him my way. After a couple of whiskey sours, he and I had concluded that we both had a ton in common. Hell, we even lived within 10 miles of each other. The group meeting went well between both sides of each of our organizations. Everyone had very positive outlooks on our future business together. My new regional president buddy, Mike, said goodbye and to keep him in mind the next time I had something going on. We would have our wives come and enjoy a night out next visit.

Well, wouldn't you know it, Mike and his wife happened to be free for the weekend of the Trans-Siberian concert. In fact, they had always wanted to see the band live. This was aligned perfectly. My bosses loved when the sales reps hung out with people on the executive level. Gaining experience and making better relationships with higher decision makers. Never mind the fact that I had only met Mike once prior to me inviting he and his wife to our event. It was going to be a nice evening of good food and interesting music. Right near the holidays to boot.

As it turned out, another friend who was a client could also make it. Rival client of the big corporate group, but he would fit in well with Mike and his wife. Of course, as always in life, not everything always goes as planned. My life is a living example of that.

As we were nearing the week from our concert, I did the customary reaching out to the committed clients to make sure schedules did not change. I needed to verify they were all still coming. Mike was the first to respond that he and his wife already had it on the calendar and were looking forward to a fun night out. My other buddy, Chas, got back to me a little later that day. He usually had me on speed dial and was always available. I knew something was up when he didn't immediately text me back. He said he was sorry, but something had come up and he had to bail on his tickets. He meant to tell me the prior week, but he was away in France, conducting some secondary job business, and had limited connectivity with the world. I could tell he felt bad. I gave him some friendly shit but told him I would find a replacement. No harm, no foul.

I had to find two replacements, and quick. I had exactly five days to make it happen. It should have been easy, but my other good client buddies were busy, out of town, or just did not give two fucks about going to a fancy dance orchestra. I didn't want the tickets to go to waste, so I then started inviting my personal friends who lived around town.

Most of them were also predisposed of, except for my good buddy Murray. He happened to be coming home from reserve drill and could probably make the end of our planned dinner, but at worse he would for sure make the concert. He was professional and he cleaned up well. I could also count on him to not go overboard or become a distraction. He could generally handle his liquor. Now I had one more ticket to find a body for. My other local friends were also disposed of or not in town.

As it turned out I ended up finding another business client to give the last ticket to. This business contact, Bradley, had been nice and loyal to me since the day I arrived in Denver. He introduced me to people around town in our business world. He was always helpful, and we never had any unpleasant interactions. However, my buddy Bradley also had a long history of drug and alcohol dependency that he had kicked for years before I met him. When I was working with him, he was on the sober side of life. I was naïve to the ways of hard drugs, or even being around someone on them. Marijuana and magic mushrooms were the crux of my hard-core drug knowledge. What I also did not know was that when I reached out to Bradley, that he was going through a major life problem. He was also dealing with that problem with the only way he knew how. Dependency. He lived right near the concert venue. Because of his personal issue he was available that day and looking forward to a good concert and some free booze.

My wife and I got to dinner a little early and Mike and his wife were just behind us. The four of us got things started before the others could join. It was a great mixer so far and we all were clicking on so many levels. Which was great for business aspect but was even better for meeting genuinely wonderful human beings.

My buddy Murray was the next person to show up. Almost an hour from concert time, but enough time that let Mike and his wife comfortably get to know him. Murray also showed up straight out of reserves, with his dress uniform on. He didn't have a choice, he didn't have time to go home and change. Mike loved that Murray was in the Navy. Mike's father was retired from the Navy. The booze was now flowing, and we were all getting along perfectly.

I knew something was up when Bradley was answering his texts very slowly. His answers didn't make a lot of sense either. He ended up meeting us at the restaurant with about 20 minutes until the show.

After a couple of last cocktails Bradley was welcomed with open arms. He was also high as fuck. Some may have noticed more than others, but at least there was nothing majorly awkward about it. Murray was way more reserved and was always quick to judge. He had questioning looks about the newcomer. What helped was that Murray knew what to expect from a Chance party. He decided to ignore the newest arrival and just go with the flow.

Mike was smitten with Bradley. He knew the business side that Bradley had run for years within their industry. He quickly took to him and aptly nicknamed him "Subprime". It was now time to head into the main event, the reason we were all here. Ava and Mike's wife took the lead and the boys followed closely behind.

The concert was a blast. We all kept up a healthy amount of alcohol consumption. There was one tiny little hiccup. About 20 minutes after the intermission, we lost "Subprime". He was doing well most of the concert. I noticed he retreated a little from us and didn't partake in some of the drinking, but overall, he was jamming to the band. Then, out of nowhere, he went to the bathroom and never came back. I think, now that he is living a sober life, he just decided to ride the Dragon and that didn't work out on coming back to the party. It was obvious to everyone else that he went missing but the group decided that he probably had something to do. All good.

After the concert ended, we all decided that it was super early. It wasn't even dinner time yet. We all had stuff to do in the morning, but we decided that we could at least grab some dinner and then plan from that point. Murray had been up since the break of dawn or earlier. He was wiped out and said that if it were a weekend night, he would have been in. So, he left us, and still no sign or word from "Subprime". The four of us left all moseyed over to the tavern across the street from the concert arena.

The tavern we were going to, as well as the concert venue we just left, was near Mile High stadium. The Broncos happened to be playing that day. The football game also happened to coincidently end around the same time as our concert. Now you had hundreds of dressed up concert goers heading to the same bar the Broncos fans were heading to. It was a recipe for an interesting end to the night.

We got into the bar. The place was packed. The outflow of the concert and the Broncos fans flooding the bar was overwhelming. As luck would have it, we found a table downstairs that had just become available. My wife sat down with Mike and his wife. As they were about to look over what to order I realized it was a great opportunity for me to use the men's room and freshen up a bit. It should be a quick in and out. My wife and newfound friends would come to find out that it would be a lot quicker than expected.

As I happily headed back to the men's restroom, I encountered the dreaded line from hell. It wasn't as bad as it could have been, but it was already outside the entrance door. There were around 10 guys in line ahead of me. My bladder was starting to feel like it was floating. The line went quick. I made it inside the men's room and was able to relieve myself. Then I heard some clamor up near the entrance where I just had come from. It was a Broncos fan, and he was belligerent and bellowing at the top of his lungs. I can't even remember the crap spewing out of this guy's mouth. Just that he was "that guy" and had to tell every single person in the room why he should be the head coach of the Broncos. Most everyone just ignored his attempt to gain attention but that was making him irater.

As I was washing my hands and looking around at the full restroom, I noticed I was one of the few people not in Broncos orange. I didn't get the chance to drop off my suit jacket, so I am one of the very over-dressed people around me. This belligerent drunk decides that because I was standing out in the crowd that he would single me out to fuck with.

He starts out by calling me a name that I can't even remember. It was slurred so bad that it didn't even make sense. It was enough to get my attention though. Even with my healthy buzz, I was not in any mood to play along with this idiot. I just smiled, nodded my head, and kept to myself which did not go over well with Bronco boy. As I went to leave, I unfortunately had no option but to pass right in front of this intoxicated individual. When I tried to pass by him, he decided to grab me by my coat to get my full attention.

This guy was drop dead drunk. He was barely enunciating every other word correctly. He was also using the wall behind him as his literal crutch. He tried pulling me a little closer. My patience was wearing ultra-thin at this point. Still though, it's not like I hadn't experienced this stupidity in my previous days. I soldier on knowing I can take this guy if need be. I was not in the fighting mood. As I removed his hand from my coat his true anger started to show itself.

"Hey, you are that fucker that I was talking about at the game!" he asked someone in thin air right next to me.

I tried to explain to this guy that I had no clue who what he was talking about. It was not working. This guy's brain had probably stopped working in the second grade. I pointed out that I was clearly not dressed for the Broncos game. I root for the Broncos. I go to many games. I have my typical jersey and such that I wear, kind of like him. The simple facts were not sinking in with this guy's logic. Nothing was working.

Let me remind you that I have been gone now about 2 minutes. I had just left my wife with a brand-new client and his wife and they were all waiting on me to come back to order some food.

I should also confess a little something here. That job I had? The one that brought me here this night? Yeah, the low pay, the long hours and the stress that job caused were building up every single day. It pushed every boundary in my life. Boundaries that did not need to be pushed that far. My wife knew this first hand. While she is an awesome confidant, I tried to limit my frustration about the job when I was with her. I wanted to focus on the positives and fun in our relationship. Of course, bottling up those feelings only gets you in a deeper emotional hell. This fateful night was a great example of why you should not bottle up major pain points in your life.

This ignorant jack hole had gone too far. As I was pulling away from him and throwing his grabbing hand back in his face, he decided our discussion was over. He threw one of the worst telegraphed haymakers I had ever seen. I felt like Neo in the Matrix dodging his drunken punch.

I was able to easily dodge his punch and grab his arm at the same time. However, he did lean his weight into it and his other hand was around my coat and he was pushing me backwards through the men's room swinging door. We barely missed a waiter with a tray full of food. I was going into full on defense and survival mode.

What came next was straight from the back of my mind that had been stored for years. My second grade Judo sensei would be proud. At the same time, I was coming back to a normal stance was about the same time I decided to sweep the leg. Well, more like just kick his lead leg, near the knee. This guy went down faster than a heavy bag of rocks.

The next part was mostly a blur as it was so quick. There happened to be another bystander to the right side of the men's room door that saw and heard the entire ordeal unfold. This gentleman must have had more pent up anger than me. That or maybe a full bottle of whiskey rolling through his body. The next thing I saw was this stranger jump in front of me and deliver three or four kicks to Bronco dudes head while he was on the ground. I had zero clue who this random bystander was. Fate has a funny way of dealing life's cards that way. I didn't ask for any help, nor did I need it. Yet there it was.

The commotion was attracting everyone around us, especially the bouncers. The staff had called out to them the second this drunko had pushed me through the men's door. The bouncers saved my ass that night. Because as I dropped the guy to the ground, he ended up blocking the outflow of the men's swinging door. Now with blood streaming down his face he was lying motionless. This guy's seven-foot mammoth friend, that had been trying to stop his buddy from doing anything, was blocked on the other side of the men's room door. The guy that had done the kicking was already walking towards the front entrance. He never exchanged a single word with me or anyone around us. The bouncers didn't care to hear a single word from myself or the guy on the ground.

The wait staff and bouncers were now yelling myself and the guy on the ground who was starting to get up. "Get out of here!! The cops are on their way!!" I didn't get any chance to respond. I was already getting neck hugged by one of the largest bouncers I had ever seen. Which was not my main concern. My concern was about to abruptly come into view.

The bouncer dragged me past the table that my wife and my new-found executive friend and his spouse were sitting at. There was nothing I could do but acknowledge them as I was dragged by. I do remember asking the bouncer to drop me off at the table and I would grab my wife and go. The bouncer had different plans. I think I was able to squeak out something about explaining later, and that I was sorry the night had to end like this. The utter amazement on the eyes of all those three was probably the funniest look a group has ever given me.

The bouncer threw me out the front door and not so politely told me to not come back anytime soon. He also let me know that I had minutes before the cops would be pulling up. Luckily my wife knew that look I gave her as I was being dragged past their table. She had told Mike and his wife that she was sorry the night had to end but she had to attend to her delinquent husband. When I whipped around to yell something at the bouncer, she grabbed me by the arm and told me that we had no time left. She was not going to deal with the police.

As we were walking across the huge parking lot, I started to explain that the situation was not my fault. Suddenly, I heard a booming voice yelling my name from behind me. It was Mike, running out to say something to me. My head was making up every possible terrible scenario that could happen here. I was thinking this night was going straight to my boss's boss and then some. It would at least be an interesting way to end this shitty job. I was always trying to make the best out of bad situations.

"Chance! Chance! I wanted to tell you that my wife and I had an awesome time! We also just saw the guy come out of the back of the bar. The cops are cuffing him up as we speak. You are the man!!! Talk to you this week!" Mike bellowed across the parking lot.

As we solemnly drove home, my wife was able to put it all together with my story. I don't know if she was happier that she didn't have to bail me out of jail, or the fact that I was not going to lose my job. Either way it was one of the rare instances on my part that we can look back and laugh.

First impressions are always key.

Having a bachelor party after a divorce makes much more sense than having it before the wedding. ~ Anonymous

WORST. SPEECH. EVER.

Wedding speeches given by the someone in the wedding party are a tradition that goes back to the Pagan ages. Some are witty, some are brash, some are heart felt tugs, some are drop dead hilarious, and then there is the all too common train wreck ones. We are talking about the spotlight being in front of the speaker and the utter nonsense they are spewing is offending even their own family. That type of train wreck speech. Most of us have been in that position or will be there in the future. I say good luck to them and know that they should realize that it is not the end of the world when you bomb a wedding speech. It really could be worse. Not much worse. But fractionally worse.

This here is all about one of those train wrecks.

Graduation from high school is one of those weird, awkward occurrences in most of our lives. On one hand you are now a Bonafede adult in the eyes of the law and the eyes of your parents. You are free to go buck wild. Some young adults will go straight into the workforce, some will take a long vacation, some will choose to move on to higher education.

So many free will choices, none of which are wrong. However, some of those choices can take you down a wrong path.

Regardless of choice, it is generally a time of reckoning. Young adults also usually get the inevitable "Oh shit, I am on my own. Everything is on me." feeling. That shit hits you damn quick. Most often we don't understand that it's usually ok. We have a support system in our family, friends, or we find a way to provide and fend for ourselves. It is that animal instinct that makes you survive and keep moving along. It also makes you feel a little confident. Sometimes a little over confident, kind of like you can say and do what you want, even though generally that couldn't be further from the truth. Real world. Real consequences.

I was all of one year removed from high school. Many of my good friends had stayed together in our hometown. A few had gone into the military or were about to leave for the military. Chris was a very close friend and he was also about to be the first in our group to get married. Chris and I had been through thick and thin growing up. In high school we became even closer, pretty much like brothers. We had the same thought process about approaching life and we both loved doing the same activities. I was not really in any awe when he told me that he popped the question to Adair. They would also be moving to Hawaii right after the wedding. The only good news was that it was going to be a fun party. Much of our longtime group of friends was still intact and in town for their wedding date. So at least there was a silver lining to losing my buddy in so many ways.

Because of our closeness in friendship I figured Chris would eventually bring up me being his best man for their wedding. It was possible that George would be asked as well. Either way we would be standing right next to each other. When Chris finally asked me to be his best man, it was half expected, half an honor. It was a big deal for him, and he asked me to be there by his side to celebrate. Of course, I agreed with a simple "hell yeah". I had about three months of prep time to fulfill my best man duties. Which were all taken care of except one very large, very important part. The typical best man speech.

I am the "off the cuff" or "on the fly" type of personality. Always have been, probably always will be. It was only in my late 30's that I found a way to combat that type of personality trait. But this era that we are discussing was way before I figured that out about myself. I was a sophomore in college. I was acting like an adult. I made the rules of my own life. Which for right or wrong, should be true of every single emerging young adult. However, that ideology, would backfire in dramatic fashion in this story.

The wedding day had arrived. They had a nice little service out at a picturesque little white chapel. The service went over without a hitch. I didn't forget the ring, the groomsmen were all exhibiting great behavior, especially for our group. It probably helped that our parents and close friends' parents were almost all in attendance. Our parents knew each other, but their main tie was that all of us had been lifelong friends. They all watched our group grow up before their eyes. Now the adult world was starting to call.

Let me take a small step backwards in this story. Let me give you the Cliffs Notes version of Chris and his bride-to-not-be and her background. They met in our junior year of high school. They had now been dating for about two years and had met while working together. It was at the local McDonalds where their love affair started. It's important to take note of this.

Like most of young, high school romances go, it was par for the course. Some fights and drama here and there. Some back and forth on the break up and make up. It was when Chris decided to sign on as a Marine that they decided it was shit or get off the pot time. On the pot they went! She was willing to drop her current job and move to Hawaii to support his blossoming Marine career.

Everything was right in the world on that sunny, blue-sky, day. The vows were perfect, and the ceremony was over. It was right after our group pictures that the limo came and picked up the entire wedding party.

The era and climate that in western Montana during this wedding was a much simpler time. There was not much to do and not much in the way of entertainment. The great outdoors was what we had. That also meant that luxury items, that people in populous states had enjoyed for years, were almost non-existent in the wild northwest. While Los Angeles had over 1,000 limos able to rent in their city, Missoula had one limo company in the entire county, which only had three limos in availability.

When we got in that limo, we were all kids in a candy store. Except that candy turned out to be champagne, and there was a lot of it. We immediately popped the corks on the first three bottles and then we raised our glasses and celebrated the newly minted couple. It was a mere half hour from the church to the reception party. We took that full half hour, plus maybe another 45 minutes riding around our hometown, wherever we wanted, because we were enjoying the rarity of riding around in a limo with unlimited booze at our young adult discretion. Which proved to be my ultimate downfall that night. I think it was when I was drinking straight from the champagne bottle that the path was set and was not able to be altered. I wasn't alone in over imbibing in our ride. George was right there with me. But his professional drinking lifestyle was far more experienced than mine.

When we got to the reception I was stumbling into the main hall. We were also noticeably late. Many of the moms came up to us with feigned laughter and then cordially asked our group where the hell we had been. It only took a couple of words and our breath for all of them to crinkle their noses in unison. With somewhat disgust and motherly disapproval, they figured out why we were late. "Bunch of drunk idiots" might, or might not have been, a comment overheard near this conjuncture. I can't be held accountable for the exact details as I was a little beyond remembering everything with exact detail during that time frame. That's why our great family and friends have generously told the rest of the story you are about to read.

As our mothers and friends took their seats, the stand in DJ did the formal announcement that the groom and bride had arrived. When it was time, we all decided it would be fun to make some sort of funny entrance. A dance. A wave. A shout out. We should have not done that. I am pretty sure we all came off as overly dressed adults with zero body control, rhythm, or public awareness.

We all took our seats and began the process of the typical wedding format. The DJ did the best he could, He was a buddy of ours that had gone home and brought his home stereo and microphone. The original DJ had bailed at the last second. So, our buddy did some intros of the wedding party and then started playing the typical wedding songs. He of course got the crowd to do the conga line. While most of us, especially myself, enjoyed the great number of friends and family that came out to enjoy the celebration, we were also continuing to enjoy the very free refreshment bar. It was wide open.

About two hours after we initially got to the venue it was time to finally do the bridesmaids and groomsmen speeches. Since we had a DJ on loan, the actual timelines the bride had planned for were a bit off. Just like much of the wedding party. It was also unfortunate that I was the best man and I was slated to speak right after the maid of honor. Before us was the other bridesmaid and groomsmen though. I was on deck but had no wits about me.

Now let me be the first (and probably only one) to defend myself here. I had known Chris for almost the entirety of my life. We hung in the same circle of miscreants and were about as close to brothers as it gets. Also, in my defense was that this was my first time being a best man. I had no clue what the hell was truly expected of me. I should also probably mention that I did have a somewhat heartwarming and endearing speech that I had prepared. But it was never written down, and it would not have mattered, as the amount of champagne and booze was all coming to a head. The train wreck was in full motion and everyone around me was "all aboard" whether they wanted to be or not.

There is not a whole lot I can remember about what was said in full context and clarity. Trust me. I really wanted this chapter to simply be titled "Worst Speech Ever" and give you all a URL to plug in that would take you straight to YouTube video of what I am about to patch together. I also make this promise. If that video does surface one day (and I know there is at least one version somewhere), I promise I will make it publicly available. I am not above my own self degradation.

I believe that my buddy George was the first to give a toast. It was probably short, sweet, and to the point. It should have also been a glaring example of what I should have followed up on. Next, I think was the maid of honor, whom we affectionately dubbed "never cry wolf" simply because of her glaring back tattoo of a howling wolf. She got up and said her somewhat long, overdrawn, but very affectionate speech to her best friend. Now it was my turn to rock the mic. It was also about then that the after effects of multiple Fireball shots coupled with bottles of champagne kicked in full throttle. Did I also mention this was my very first best man speech?

What was told to me by multiple family members and friends in attendance as well as the bride's side of the family, was that they heard the worst wedding speech in the history of mankind.

I know I started out, or at least wanted to start out, with something sentimental. But I was 18, stone cold drunk, and past the point of return. I simply started out by cussing about everything that was going through my head. Something like "Well guys and gals. This is the fucking end of this friendship. My man Chris has done fucked up and gotten locked down with the old ball and chain."

The crickets chirping in the room were enough of a dead giveaway that I should have stopped right then and there. The devil on my shoulder prodded me to keep on going. I then decided to go ahead and tell the entire room how they proceeded to meet. Apparently, I said something to the tune of "I remember when these two love birds fucking met. They had been working their asses off over at the local Micky D's and Chris had been swatting Adair's ass with the spatula they were using to flip burgers for their customers. It was love at first sight. Soon they were both fucking on top of the grill after hours and the rest is history."

That was one of those rare moments when the phrase "you could cut the tension in the air with a knife" came from. Adair and I already didn't care for one another. She was taking my buddy away, and I was in her way of full control of Chris. The anger and astonishment from her alone was one for the books. It was also probably one of the few times my mom just buried her head in her hands while wondering how she could legally disown me. Think any of that stopped the onslaught of a good ol' Chance's speech? Nope. The train kept on rolling along. I at least got a few nervous chuckles from somewhere in the audience.

I guess I might have rattled off some stats about Chris after that. Something to the tune about his love of gangsta rap, maybe even a quote of two from a Geto Boys album. I don't know. Time and consciousness had slipped well beyond me at that point. By that time the audience all had mouths wide and were gasping at everything I was saying. I assumed, incorrectly, that I was in the zone. I had this audience by the balls, and they loved me! Looking back, I think it was more of my muddled mind trying to rationalize the guilt it felt for me.

I pretty much ended the whole thing with a recap of their sexual exploits they liked to do around me. They always thought it was kinky to have sex in the same room when we would all be together. I assumed it was fair game to let their family members know that as well. I think in my mind I was just being funny, but the fear from their mother's eyes should have told me more.

It was right about when I was going to wrap up with a bang, that one of my buddies, Frank, decided to save me. Well, to be honest, he was just wanting to save the rest of the room the embarrassment of me. So, he stood up, raised his glass, and bellowed out my childhood nickname, "Alright Floyd! Have another, buddy!" It was at that moment, when the audience started clapping and I saw my mother with tears in her eyes, that I knew I had slayed that crowd. I was the biggest hit since Sinatra made his famous wedding speech at Sammy's wedding. I can only wait to be asked to be all my buddies' weddings and assume best man speech duties.

It was the next day, when I woke up in the bathroom of the house I was staying at, literally curled up around the toilet, that some flashbacks began occurring. There was the flashback of my ex-girlfriend telling me off. There was the flashback of all my friends asking me "what the fuck were you thinking?" Then there was that lasting impression of my mother telling me I need to stop drinking and maybe move to a remote country for a little while. That is when I knew my dream of being a stand-up comedian or a professional wedding speaker was never going to happen.

Let me tell you this my friends. Failure is only the first step towards success. Do not let the ghosts of yesterday become the reason you stop reaching for your dreams. Admittingly, "the worst wedding speech ever" did follow me around for many, many years. Surprisingly, I did not get asked to make a speech at any of the weddings I was in for about 20 years. But when I finally did, I nailed it. That is another chapter I will share with you all on a different page and a different year. Now where did I put that bottle of champagne?

THE $87,612 PEARL JAM TICKET

I love to travel. I also love to travel to see some of my favorite musicians perform in unique venues. I guess if I had it my way and had money to spare, I would become a professional concert groupie. Not for one unique band, but more for unique venues. It could be anyone that I loved playing said venue.

As it currently stands, I have seen some amazing bucket list bands and luckily some of them before they passed on to the Rock and Roll Hall of Fame in the big blue sky. I have also been blessed to see a pantheon of legendary venues, from the famed Red Rocks Amphitheater outside of Denver to the Grand Ole Opry in Nashville and the City Park in downtown New Orleans. A wide vestibule of history-making concerts from all eras and genres of bands.

This story took place in the not so distant past. It needs to be told because the events leading up to it are so unreal and I am very lucky and blessed to even be writing these words.

One of my favorite bands, and one that I had seen play live seven times prior in the last 20 years, happened to announce they were going to play only seven shows (originally it was supposed to be five, but they changed to seven right after the initial announcement) in the US, during 2018. It was Pearl Jam. They decided they would dub the very short tour the "Home Shows" tour. Two shows in Seattle, one show in Missoula, two shows in Chicago, then the last two shows in Boston. All would take place in outdoor stadiums, even the one in Montana. All cities are where members of the band currently live. After the home shows they would not be touring for the foreseeable future. New album development time.

It was almost perfect. They would be coming through in the middle of August to Missoula. Better yet, they had a way of making sure their fans would have a high chance at getting tickets. It was part of their Ten club program which would also make sure all seats were equally priced and every club member would get a chance at getting great seats for that low price. Even better was that they were playing on a Monday night. So, while this single show would sell out, there were multiple mitigating factors that made it easier to get the tickets.

The only part that turned out not perfect was that I had the dates of my personal life mixed up. I had every intention of making it a work trip as Wyoming and Montana were part of my sales territory, but I also had every intention of getting my wife up to the concert with myself and my buddies. That was not to be. Her first week of teaching started that exact week. So did my son's first day of second grade. No way around those dates being missed. While my wife was bummed, she at least could revel in the fact she got to see show number seven with me in Denver. It was a classic Pearl Jam show, and we ended up with great seats to that prior show. She was all for me still going and making a boys' homecoming trip around the concert.

The day came to buy tickets and for once, my fan status on something actually worked. I was able to buy the allotted max of four tickets through advance presale and buy them at face value. $400 later I knew that my friends and I were in for a great four-day weekend. My buddy Frank was in. He already lived in Missoula and didn't have to worry about securing his own show ticket. Our close buddy, Wookie, was also in. Even before he talked to his wife and before he checked his work schedule. The last time he saw us all he was coming off a successful round of battling cancer. He was currently winning the battle, but he was also coming back from many battle scars from his three-year fight. This was a great way to escape some of that reality. Then it came to our good buddy George. Unfortunately, George was now a very responsible adult. Long gone were the days of "Fun Bobby (Friends TV show reference)". Now the new, and vastly improved, George had emerged. While this was a huge personal win in his life, it was also a sad dent in us getting the band back together again. There was no budging George. He was into church every Sunday, and House Hunters every weekday evening. He wasn't going to give either of those up for some stupid band he didn't like. He actually liked Pearl Jam's music. What he did not like was Eddie Vedder voicing his opinions. George also unfortunately fell for every Russian Facebook trick in 2016 and 2017. The Russkies got good old George. No issues. A good friend of mine from Denver, who wanted to see Pearl Jam badly, was able to make the trip work. Date and times were set.

The week of my travel was about to start. The tickets were printed out and I was able to get my son off to second grade in style. I had two days in Denver to finish up some client work, then I would travel through Wyoming for two days and then be in Montana by the end of the week to finish up the work portion of the trip and begin the get together with the boys.

Monday afternoon I decided to grab a burrito for lunch. I grabbed one from a pretty large chain, one known to be more of a fresh fixings, healthier fair. They unfortunately also had a few years of bad press with some large Salmonella outbreaks. That has never been enough to deter me. That afternoon I thought that the movie, Final Destination, had caught up with me. Immediately after my delicious burrito was finished, I felt an odd feeling. Now, mind you, I have had food poisoning before. It's no joke and there is no controlling it. This was not the same. I don't know how to explain it so that you understand. My body, and mainly my guts, just felt wrong.

I put a mental note on that and moved on with daily life. By the end of the night my body overall still felt off, but other than some tightening in the top of my abdomen, I felt fine. No nausea. No ill effects.

On Tuesday I awoke pretty much the same way. No pain. No issues. Just a little tighter in the top part of my abdomen. I went about my usual day, worked out in the morning and then finished up a lot of my client work as I was going to be traveling for the next week. By the end of Tuesday night, I was starting to feel a difference in my body. While nothing crazy, that tightness in my abdomen had now become a dull ache on the verge of a pulled muscle type of feeling. I looked up Salmonella poisoning on the internet and the symptoms matched up with some of mine. Not a perfect match though. The description also told me that there is pretty much nothing I could do to fix it. It is a "ride it out and hope you don't die" type of virus.

So, on Wednesday I got up and the symptoms were in the "getting very painful" stage. No workout that day. I drop off my daughter, tell her to be good for mom for the next week, and then start my work trips up the east side of Wyoming. All the while dealing with this perceived Salmonella poisoning while interacting with clients.

I got through my Cheyenne and Casper clients with ease. Other than me saying something to them, they had no clue that I was going through anything. I was doing better than I thought so I decided I would push it and stay in Sheridan, Wyoming that night. Maybe I could get through my clients early enough on Thursday and then be able to make a late trek to Montana to make it home to Missoula sooner than anticipated.

That night I found an amazing steak house and was happy to get an awesome meal and some local mead. My stomach however was having nothing to do with it. I only got about half the sandwich down and a couple of beers. While there was no nausea or diarrhea happening, there was a definite loss of appetite going on. I also did something rare for me: I went to bed early.

I woke up early Thursday morning and the pain seemed to be getting worse. The Ibuprofen was not cutting it. The pain also seemed to have shifted from the top of my abdomen to the bottom right of my abdomen. This all seemed great in my opinion. I got up earlier than anticipated, ate a light breakfast and got to see my clients in town.

I only made it through one. It was at the end of that meeting that the pain became more intense and had shifted back to the top of my abdomen. It was enough to really make me take note. It had been three days straight of increasing pain. It was time to really think about getting this looked at. Even if it's Salmonella and it can't be rectified. I just needed it evaluated.

At that point I decide I can make it to Billings, Montana. I would stop and see a good friend if he was in town, and evaluate my body and the pain, at that next stop. Luckily, he was in. It was a brutal two-hour drive from Sheridan to Billings. The reprieve of getting up and not being slumped over in my car seat was fantastic.

I got to catch up with my buddy and do some work as well. When I mentioned my issues the past few days, my buddy just kind of laughed it off. Then he told me in a serious tone, "You might just have a leaking or burst appendix. I went through that when I was younger, and it was brutal." I told him I already thought of that and looked up the symptoms. The problem was that it had been hurting in my upper abdomen and not down to the right like what the internet and people had described. We exchanged goodbyes and I was getting on the road to head home. There was a little relief from the pain but about an hour into the drive I got a pretty big jolt that would stop me in my tracks.

I knew that I wanted to take a little detour on my way back to Missoula. Even though the pain had come back and was more than the previous three days, I wanted to run through Livingston, Montana and head to the little town south of there called Gardiner. It was the north entrance of Yellowstone Park and it was also a place I had targeted in a treasure hunt that I was pursuing. Forrest Fenn. Look him up.

As I got into Livingston, I knew I also needed to scope out any Urgent Cares in town. Luckily there was one and it was right across from an Albertsons grocery store. I needed to desperately use a bathroom. I also needed something that might help me take a shit. I hadn't had one of those since Monday and it was now Thursday and that was very abnormal for my body.

Instead of calling my company's TeleNurse service, or my mom who was a retired thirty-year CTN, or even my father in law, a general practitioner, I decided on good old' George. There was a rhyme to that reason. George is a master shitter. Homeboy takes about four dumps a day, on the regular. He also used to map out the best bathrooms around our hometown because his bowels could surprise him at any given moment. I called him as I was gingerly walking through the grocery store. I explained my issue and my weird amount of days of bowel backup. He prescribed me a soft stool relaxer. He said if it was a gastric problem, this certain over-the-counter drug would be the right one to fix it. The expert spoketh.

I purchased his suggested stool softener and then decided that it was time to take the 50-mile drive to Gardiner. I wanted to explore for the multi-million dollar treasure some crazy old man possibly hid in that area. It took all of 15 miles outside of Livingston for that plan drastically change. My stomach went from painful to burning hell in that very short drive. I flipped a U-turn faster than Michael Schumacher took a curve in the Grand Prix. It was honestly the worst 15 mile drive I have ever experienced. Which is saying a lot as I have driven through the Dakotas. I was also silently cursing out George. It had been about 30 minutes since I took his recommended medicine dosage and I swore that the burning pain was associated with his suggestion.

I finally got back into Livingston and luckily the Urgent Care was right on that side of town. I could barely hobble myself to the front door. My guess was that I looked like a 90-year-old man that just had stomach surgery. The front desk lady and the other patrons sitting in the waiting room looked at me with empathy, but also with that side glance of "what the fuck is wrong with this guy?" I explained my issues with the lady at the front and she took my info and said I would be seen very soon.

I only had to wait about ten minutes for the attending nurse and doctor to see me. Thank god for little towns and low populations. As I struggled to get up, I noticed this teenage girl get wheeled out of the back room. Her father and brother were in the front lobby waiting on her. The mom who was wheeling her calmly told the dad that they need to move on to the local hospital. The daughter had appendicitis. As I was slowly walking back to the ER room, I found it humorous that my buddy had mentioned appendicitis only a couple hours prior. Weird how the strange paths seem to work in this mysterious world.

I was on the medical bed no longer than a minute before the attending nurse popped in. She asked me what was going on. I explained that I thought I had Salmonella poisoning from a bad burrito three days prior, but that I knew my body, and something was majorly off. She took my basic vitals and quickly concurred. She rushed out to grab the attending physician. He quickly came in, got the full story and full details and then did some basic tests on me which included a lot of poking and prodding. Unfortunately for both of us, he poked the wrong spot at the wrong time.

That medicine that my buddy prescribed me? It was now 40 minutes into me taking it and the effects seemed to be working. That prod the attending gave me had just released the first fart I had in over 3 days. Rancid is a great word to describe the putrid smell that was quickly filling the small room. The big release my stomach just let out reminded me briefly of life without stomach pain. It also gave my attending doc the face of a man who wished he was in a cotton candy factory as opposed to this specific ER room.

He was sold, or maybe he just wanted me gone. After his deductions he knew that he did not have the resources to help me. He needed to send me 12 miles away to the local hospital. They were better equipped to diagnose me fix my problem. They had updated medical equipment more experienced staff. They asked if I was going to need an ambulance and I promptly told them no. I was convinced I was already on the verge of the ultimate horrible insurance bill. Even though I had insurance, I just assumed that I was out of network. Life was more important than money at this point, but I knew I could make that miserable trip faster than in an ambulance.

I shuffled my broken body to my car and drove the 12 miles to the hospital. When I pulled into the ER parking lot, I noticed this was a brand-new hospital. I was contemplating risking the 25-mile drive to Bozeman, which I knew was a much larger city and probably had newer facilities, but my abdomen gave me a reassuring sharp reminder. I barely made it here, there was no more extra miles left in me.

I did my best Yoda impression as I slunk my way slowly through the ER entrance and to the front desk. The Urgent Care crew had called over so the lady at the front desk knew who I was. As I entered, I noticed the same family that I had just seen leave Urgent Care before I went in. The teenage daughter did not look well at all. "Poor girl." I thought to myself. I bet they were headed to Yellowstone as well. What bad luck to have your appendix burst while on a family vacation. That would really suck. Not that Salmonella poisoning was much better.

I was quickly escorted to one of the back emergency rooms. It was then that two things stood out to me. The first thing was not highly un-usual. The entire staff in the back was women. I did not see one single male. The second thing I noticed was that everyone was young. Fresh out of college young. Each of these young women were also very good looking. I thought that odd as Livingston was a small, out in the mid-dle of nowhere, town. I later would find out that this happened to be a training medical center. All the new grads were sent here. My luck was running out.

Two of the nurses came back and got my story. They also did the obligatory "Please disrobe and get into your gown that is made of tracing paper." They helped me lay down and started taking my vitals as well as putting an IV in me.

Let me say something before I get to the last parts of this story. A huge thank you to all the nurses and caretakers out there. You have to put up with people who are generally at their worst. You also must see and smell things that most people do not experience in their entire lives. The doctors, they come and go. Give a diagnosis and they are out. But the nurses out there? You stay for the long haul and are the true champions. I give each one of you reading this a giant virtual hug and kiss. You are doing work that is truly exemplary. I also apologize for what we patients can do, not by our own accord, but that our body makes us do.

Fucking George and his dumbass television medical skills. It was now over an hour since I took his recommended medicine. I was laying on my back, with multiple hot young nurses coming in and out of my teeny tiny room. That is when Georges medical advice kicked in. The Kraken that was growing in my guts the last 3 days decided it was time to show its existence.

Right as two new nurses walked in, I released what could only be described as the mother of all farts. It was a room clearer. I was mortified, yet also temporarily relieved. Thank god those ladies had probably seen it all. They attended to me, in that mustard gas filled room, as if it was just another day. I did notice one of them do the "stop breathing through your nose" technique that is often deployed in similar situations. There was absolutely nothing I could do to stop nature and medicine from exacting their revenge. The deadly gas coming out of me did not stop. Of course, neither did the change in nurses that had to help me.

I must have been one of the few patients in the hospital that day. Both the main parking lot and ER parking lot were void of cars when I drove in earlier. I would take a wild guess that was why I was introduced to the entire nursing staff that day. They, unfortunately, were introduced to 3 or more days of bile buildup from my stomach. It kept going. That small, side room in the ER had to smell like the cow farm smell that hits you when driving into Greeley, Colorado.

They did a CAT scan and other blood tests so see what exactly was going on with my body. Nothing good came back. On top of that, my gas problem was only getting worse. Here is a little fact for you: don't ever fart in a confined CAT scan. Trust me on that one.

After my scan they moved me back into my small ER room, that unfortunately still had my lingering stench. My bloodwork came back with terrible results. My white blood count came back scary low. Like I should be dead type of low.

Right away that brought in the attending doctor, who was all of 30 years old and of course, like the rest of the entire staff, she great looking side of life. My stomach was an utter mess. The IV and antibiotic drips were not helping yet. But the morphine? Oh, that was working just fine. It was also relaxing my bowels. This poor attending doctor had no choice but to get into the trench of fartdom. I was so high from the morphine that I lost my utter embarrassment factor. The only good thing to report from that ER visit.

She told me that the scan was bad. They thought my appendix was perforated and might even be leaking. This was a twofold problem. The first issue was that my inner gut was massively inflamed. It was so inflamed that they could not get a clear picture of what was really going on. The second issue was that I was one of the rare people that had their appendix behind the colon. Usually more than 90% of people have their appendix in front of the colon.

Surgery was happening. No way around it. They informed me that if they were to do surgery right then that they were sure they would need to do incision surgery as opposed to doing a laparoscopy surgery. The good news was that going the lap surgery route would be way less invasive and would be less recovery time from the small incisions. I promptly agreed that we should go the laparoscopy route, in between very loud bombs emanating from my butt. She told me they were going to get me on the antibiotic drip for the next 24 hours. She hoped the inflammation would lessen and the probability of lapro surgery would be almost guaranteed.

My pain was still there but had started to subside with the morphine. At that time, four more nurses that had been bebopping in and out of the stinkfest room came to wheel me away to my hospital bedroom.

This gave me time to get in touch with wife as well as my family and friends to let them know what was going on. My wife of course wanted to fly into Bozeman that night. I assured her I fine and that this was an easy surgery. My parents offered to drive the four hours to my hospital and so did my in-laws. I just told everyone I loved them, and I was in good hands where I was at. Appendectomies happen all the time. This was a routine deal. No need for them to drive the long distance when I would be in and out soon enough.

The rest of that Thursday afternoon I was able to lay on my back and relax the fire going on in my stomach. The cavalcade of attending nurses, as well as doctors and case managers coming to check in on me didn't allow me much rest. They all had to hear the story of me thinking it was

Salmonella poisoning and that a leaking appendix was in no way what I thought it would be.

When the doctor who would be performing my surgery came in, he again needed to know all the facts. He wanted to know why I had been traveling so long with this pain. I told him I had a Pearl Jam concert to get to in four more days. I was already missing some fun times with my friends and family back home. I mentioned that I was trying to make it back to Missoula so that I could be taken care of by my mother and her doctor connections. The gods of disappointment decided to rain on those plans and that is why I was in a hospital bed in Livingston instead back home.

The doctor looked at me with pity and uncertainty. He told me that the surgery was planned for Friday evening so that the antibiotics could do their job. He also told me that my recovery time and stay could last well into the next week. It all depended on how the surgery played out. That sucked a little wind out of me. I was going to miss the concert of the year because of a stupid, possibly leaking appendix. How's that for some shitty luck? What could I do? It was what it was. No getting around it. The choice was life in Livingston or death by Pearl Jam.

I finally spoke with everyone I needed to in the outside world. I also finally got some peace and quiet. When I woke up later that night, I knew something was wrong. There was searing pain coming from my torso that I can't describe. The drugs were doing nothing to combat that pain.

The night nurse took forever to get to me. Which I found odd as there were not that many patients in my hospital wing. When she finally came in, I just laid it out. My pain level was in that 10 zone and I could sense that something was really, really wrong. She told me there was nothing to do but take more pain medicine and wait until morning. She would talk to the doctor about it ASAP. Then she left for the night. I wondered what happened to the plethora of training nurses that I saw a mere 12 hours earlier.

Even with the amount of "Keith Richards" drugs they were pumping through me, it was not enough to knock me out. I was up from 4 AM until the doctor came to see me around 8 AM. He asked me what was going on, did some tests, looked over my vitals and said I would be in the next ER prepped room. His non-poker face was not helping me coax through the terrible thoughts within my head.

I got into the prepped OR room and back were the hot nurses. I didn't care. I wanted the demon that was causing me severe pain to be cut out of my body. When the little old anesthesiologist came in to administer the surgery drugs I was starting to hallucinate. I was also sweating profusely. Then, everything went black.

The next thing I remembered was this nice old lady stroking my arm and head and telling me that I was coming about. It took a minute for me to remember where I was and why this stranger was helping me. The only thing she said to me was that I was now recovering from surgery and that while the surgery went well there was complications. She then told me that due to HIPAA laws that was all she could tell me and that my doctor needed to explain the rest. Who the fuck wakes someone up like that? I mean, I get the laws, but damn lady. Work on your bedside manners.

Thankfully my doctor was in the next room and was by my side within five minutes.

"So here is the deal" he sternly told me. "The operation was great, we were able to do the lapro surgery. It was indeed your appendix that was the issue. It is now gone. The problem was that you were full-on septic. That strange feeling you had five days ago? Yeah, that was your appendix bursting. There have been toxins pouring into your body the last five days. People can die from being septic within an hour. You might have broken a world record for longest days septic and still breathing. You must have some serious guardian angels or luck like no other." He had no way of knowing my past and my prior run-ins with the Grim Reaper and his friends.

It took me a few minutes to digest all that news. When I finally came back to reality, I only could think of one question. I conjectured since the surgery went so well and the fact they thought that they got most of my toxins out, that I had a good possibility of early recovery. I simply asked, since everything seemed to be in order, and I felt a shit ton better what was his professional prognosis that I would be getting out of the hospital in the next couple days? So, I could make my Pearl Jam concert?

I am pretty sure the look he conveyed was one of sympathy. I am pretty sure he thought my IQ level had dropped in tandem with the cocktail of drugs administered to my body in the last 24 hours. Why else would a patient ask such a dumb question right after they were told they were not statistically supposed to be among the living?

"Yeah, we will see how you do tonight and through the weekend. I would not get your hopes up." he chortled.

That small sentiment of positive thinking was all I needed. In fact, that amount is about all I ever need in life. Just give me the smallest maybe. I will win will that battle every time. For life. University Motors "Hubbard" chop. Inside joke there. Sorry about that.

The recovery from surgery sucks. There is no other way to put it. That Friday night was about as uncomfortable as I had ever been. It was all I could do to reach out to my friends and family and update them that I was doing fine. My body was wrecked. My mind was racing with about every ADHD thought that could possibly fit in it. I also had been talking to all my buddies that were back in Missoula. They were partying together and catching up. The depression set in with the reality that I was probably going to have to miss out on all of that.

Saturday rolled around. I really started feeling better. I was at least able to get up and walk to the bathroom on my own accord. It hurt like hell, even with the drugs, but I considered it a good omen. I even got to get into the shower and wash away two days of blood and sweat. Life was looking up even though I was all by my lonesome in this beautiful little town. I was becoming more hopeful that I was going to make it back to Missoula in time to at least catch the concert.

I had a huge problem though. I still had not been able to take a poop. Export gas? No issue there. It was not near as deadly as it was two days ago. I was now going on six days without a bowel movement and that is no Bueno. The doc had prescribed a prescription grade stool softener that I had now been taking for a full day. Still nothing was coming loose in my guts. The new concern was that they may have to go in and do a surgery for internal waste removal. Which meant there was absolutely no way of getting back home in time for the concert They did tell me they had a different option they wanted to try. I was not going to like it at all. They wanted to try an anal suppository.

Guys are straight up wussies when it comes to certain things with their body. Pain in or around our bodies is one of those weak points. We can be as tough as we want, but then we get a simple cold and we run straight to our wives, girlfriends, or mommies for emergency care. It has been that way since the dawn of time, and it will continue to be that way for many more years to come. I had reached the age where I was introduced to the "doctor finger" to check for prostate cancer. That first intrusion was not my thing. Ever. The thought of getting a giant-sized pill rammed up my butt made me cringe. My negotiating tactics went into full bloom. I convinced myself that the chance of it working or at least getting my care staff to think it was working was worth it. The things we do for the things we love. I hope you are reading this Eddie.

Around 9 PM that Saturday night, after the prescribed stool softeners were not working, in sauntered nurse Ratched with some good news. It was anal time. This duty was part of her job but there was no way she was about to enjoy what was going to go down. She tried to lighten the mood by telling me that I had a cute butt. That attempt at light hearted humor was broken by distinctive snap of her extra strength industrial plastic glove. Instinctively I started humming "Animal", which is one of my all-time favorite Pearl Jam tunes. I still have no clue why that specific tune popped into my head.

The best way to describe what happened is this. Have you ever seen a cow or horse give birth? Well what went down was that like that, but in opposite direction. There were multiple lubrication attempts. Many words yelled back and forth between us. In the end, Nurse Ratched reluctantly won. That half hour struggle was not fun for either of us. After she took off the gloves and told me not to roll over for about 10 minutes, she muttered something under her breath about not getting paid enough to do this shit. I concurred.

Sunday morning rolls around and I convince myself I feel like a rock star! I am ready to GTFO of this little town. I informed my parents that morning that I was leaving either way. They started their four hour drive out to Livingston. Sure enough, the doc saw my charts, and everything seemed to be going the right way. I also might have fibbed a bit and told him what wonders that giant cowbell shoved up my bum did for my toilet time. Stool had happened. But it really did not happen. I was not getting stuck here another night. I had pushed the amount of what this little stay had already cost me. I was still sure my insurance would find some way to pin all the costs on me.

It's also slightly possible I bribed the doctor with compliments and a heartfelt gift. I handed him a signed copy of my previous book, "The Strange Paths We All Follow" and told him I thought every person should have at least one personalized or signed book from an author in their library. Half an hour later I was magically discharged and being wheeled out to the main lobby. Unfortunately, I still had the JP still in my gut so standing up was no easy chore.

My parents were still too far out. They were about 30 minutes outside of Bozeman just driving by Wheat, Montana. I told my mom I was fine and that I needed to see what it felt like to drive. It was a short drive to Bozeman, and I needed to stop by a Walgreens there to get my prescriptions filled. Especially the pain killers. I would not advise anyone out of that type of surgery to do the same. It worked out though. I was able to meet my folks in Bozeman and my dad took my keys and drove my car so I could sleep all the way to Missoula.

That Sunday was overall uneventful. Some of my family stopped check up on me. My buddies also stopped in to give me shit. Frank promptly told me I looked like death. Dead man walking. Sometimes that saying "with friends like these . . ." really is true. At least Wookie was his usual jovial self and cracking jokes. People came and went, and I got the rest I needed. I did not move off my parents couch that day or night.

While I was laid up in my hospital bed, I was a social media Rockstar. I had all the time in the world. One person I reached out to was an old high school friend who used to be my neighbor. She knew what I was going through from Facebook updates that she caught. We got in touch and I told her I was trying to go to the concert on Monday. She promptly said something to the effect that I was crazy, but she would do what she could do. She worked at the University of Montana where the concert was being held. She got back to me when I was back home and told me that she had spoken with the head of ticketing and got my name put on the disability list for the concert.

While I had been lucky to get tickets for this sold out concert, unfortunately the seats I got ended up being on the far side of the stage and in the upper decks. Still great seats as the venue only held 25,000 people. So there really wasn't a bad seat in the house. The problem was that there was no way I would be able to get the stairs to our seats. I would also not be able to stand more than a couple minutes at a time. When Heather told me, she had hooked me up, I knew that fate was on my side.

Monday morning came quick. PJ day was here. My mom fought me tooth and nail. She swore I was being the biggest idiot she knew. I was literally three days removed from surgery and from an infection that should have killed me the first day.

I assured her that the antibiotics were working, and the painkillers were really helping. I had also secured one of those hand scooters strollers that had a comfy bench seat. That was how I was going to be able to walk to the venue and into my new seats. I swore this was all working out for a reason. She knew better than to distract the paths we are all supposed to follow. The signs were all around us. She didn't buy any of that, but she knew better than to fight me on certain things.

My last buddy in our group, Scott, came into Missoula later than expected. He was crashing at my parent's place for the night and was stoked to see his first Pearl Jam concert. A bucket list item that he was about to cross off.

He picked me up about 3 PM on Monday. He had met my parents before. When my mom scolded him for allowing me to go to this concert, he just smiled it off, drank a glass of wine with her, and promised to take good care of me. With reluctance my mom said "fine, go ahead and get yourself sick again." With those positive words of encouragement, I said my goodbyes and took my wheelie stroller and bounced out with Scott.

We stopped by a local bar and pizzeria that was only a half mile from the stadium. We needed to meet up with the rest of the crew and get the tickets and money exchanged. That took a couple hours and a few beers. By the time Scott and I decided we wanted to leave and check out the tailgate party around the stadium, I was feeling quite healthy. I was not sure if the number of stares I got in the half mile scoot to the venue was from the sight of my ghostly white body, or from the rare Mookie Blaylock jersey I was sporting. See, Pearl Jam was named Mookie Blaylock for a short time until they renamed themselves Pearl Jam. A little history for you that you never needed or wanted.

We got to the tailgate party and it was completely packed. Everyone was in party mode. We were able to secure a beer and then we decided to start the line process to get into the stadium. With my mobile scoot hindrance plus the amount of people already in line we figured we should get an early start.

Thankfully Scott was cool about everything and said he would escort me to my seat and then head back to the original seats with the others.

I was very thankful as I was feeling a little depleted of energy already. Even with the assistance this was the most I had been upright in almost five full days. We paid zero attention to the fact there were multiple lines forming. I figured it didn't matter.

It took about 25 minutes to get up to the front of the line. What is funny is both Scott and I noticed that there were people being kicked out ahead of us and being directed back to other lines. We just chose to ignore that. When it was our turn, we handed over our tickets. The look of confusion on the lady's face as well as the look of feeling sorry for me were both noticeable. She explained we were in the wrong line as this line was for the floor seats. I explained I was on the disability list and that I was told this was the line I was supposed to be in. She checked with her partner. Her friend shrugged and came over to tell us she was letting us in, but my buddy Scott was required to stay with me. For legal and support reasons. The smile on Scott's face was one of the rare things that immediately told you he just figured out what that really meant.

In my last book I mentioned something always weird seemed to happen to me at Pearl Jam concerts? Well this one was par for the course. Here I was, being escorted by the security staff, to our seats. I was merely three days out of surgery and one week to the day when my appendix ruptured. Let's not forget the fact that I should not be walking around and quite possibly should be below ground at this juncture. I still made the fucking concert. Also, our upgraded, disability seats that my friend Heather had helped me secure? Yeah. They were lower level, side stage seats. I looked to my left and up the back of the south stands where our original seats were and could only smile. Frank and Wookie were going to be pissed.

Silver linings folks. We all have them. Sometimes you just need to look below the surface. That might not be as easy to see for everyone.

But the silver linings are always there. Its perception and perspective. It's also about not giving up. I didn't give up when I was blowing death out of my ass for all those poor nurses. I thought to myself, this is going make a great story, and I can't wait to see where this ends up.

Some people take humor and see it as a burden. Some people forget the truly humorous situations they have been in because they focus on the negative. Focus on the positives in life. You are headed to the ground at some point Nothing you can do about that, it's inevitable. Why not figure out how to laugh through this crazy thing called life? Trust me. Your life will be boundlessly better.

I do leave you with this. If you find yourself with body issues that you know are not right, please go seek a professional. Not your buddy you have known for 30 some years. Who knows? It might even lead to side stage tickets to one of your favorite bands.

P.S.

Two weeks after all this happened, I had a relapse. Well, a statistical relapse. They didn't get all the toxins out of my gut and some of them attached to my new surgery spot. At least I was back in Colorado with my wife and kiddos. They all drove me to the ER which resulted in another operation. That also ended up putting me three more days and nights at the hospital. That doubled my overall medical bill. That Pearl Jam ticket just might have become the Guinness World Record price for a single ticket ever. Still worth it.

Who am I kidding? That was in no way the most expensive price paid to see an artist perform. You know there was some incredibly wealthy person that spent like $1,000,000 for Sisqó to come to their sweet 16 birthday party. That 'Thong Song' was tight.

VANITY PLATES FROM HELL

San Diego is one of the most beautiful cities in North America. Hell, I think it rivals some of the most beautiful cities in the world for that matter. When Ava and I lived in northern California we had the pleasure of having multiple friends in and around the San Diego area. It was always a wonderful weekend getaway from the cow fields and flatlands of Sacramento.

George was now living in Rancho Cucamonga, which happened to only be an hour and half drive down to San Diego. Even better, Frank was flying in from Seattle. He was overdue for his annual George time and party time with my wife and I. Ava also found out that one of her good friends and bridesmaids from college was in San Diego this same weekend. Frank and George also knew Ava's friend. We all attended college together. Frank always had a huge crush on her. Which was odd because Frank's best friend and ex roommate, Murray, had dated her. This had all the ingredients to be another crazy weekend.

Ava and I made our usual five-hour drive from Sacramento to the Inland Empire. We always liked the open road and enjoyed listening to my mixed CD's. Music, good conversation and always a stop at the In-N-Out outside of Bakersfield.

We arrived later Friday night in the Cucamonga. Frank had already gotten there, and George and his roommate had picked him up and were quite a few beers ahead of us. We were about three hours behind these jokers and needed to play catch up. Nothing big happened that night. We went to a local bar and caught up with each other and told the same stories my wife had heard over 1000 times. Most of those stories can be found within this and the prior book. Our group loved to reminisce.

The next morning was nice. Typical 80 degrees in southern California. We also had no traffic down the 15 to San Diego. You would have thought mama cooked breakfast with no hogs. You can look that reference up on your own. We were all stoked for some sun, sand, and fun. As it turned out, Ava's friend Barb, was not going to be able to meet us until dinner that night.

A little background on Barb. She was one of Ava's first friends when Ava transferred into the University of Montana. They were sorority sisters and that's how Ava and I eventually met. Not through Barb directly, but through another good friend of hers, Lorey. As mentioned earlier, Barb also ended up dating one of our group members, Murray.

Their relationship was hot and heavy until Murray got shipped off to be Lieutenant Dan in the Navy. He had an odd goal in life. He wanted to drive a submarine someday. When Murray shipped out the usual long-distance relationship tried to happen. Then some things happened in the interim that caused the relationship to sour. In all reality it was great for both Barb and Murray. Murray will probably never marry and that's not a bad thing. Some people are just destined to remain single. Zero judgement or stigma should be attached with that decision.

It also gave Barb the chance to find her one true love. It also gave our group the freedom of not paying for their ridiculous parties. They had a $25 per person cover charge for their Spaghetti-O and Francia Box-O-Wine parties. The cover charge was a 3000% price inflation. No one misses those parties.

Poor Ava. She always got stuck with the guys more often than not. By stuck I don't necessarily mean it in a bad way. She really did like George. He was entertaining in so many ways. She was starting to become closer with Frank. He had gotten a little weird with a couple of her sorority sisters back in the day. Nothing terrible, just some peculiar behavior that she figured was due to his extreme fish allergies. He also might have ruined our engagement announcement at her sorority event. She was not one to hold grudges though. When Frank was not overboard on the alcohol, he was very sweet and had a wicked funny side. This weekend he was on his best behavior. George and I, on the other hand, were a different story.

We all decided that since we had the morning and afternoon free, we would spend it down at Pacific Beach. The meatheads and bikini models were out in full force. The usual San Diego marine layer had burnt off and that glorious, perfect weather was in full display.

This was Ava and I's first trek to PB, as the locals called it. George and Frank had been down a couple times and they knew the lay of the land. Well, not really. They knew the last beach bars they had slithered into where they had the usual drunk buddy festivals. Ava got to do a little shopping on the beach. Between shops she would come have a drink with the guys. Everyone was having fun, the usual stories and jokes were being retold, and there was plenty of laughter. Just that perfect beach bum type of carefree day.

We ended up not watching the time and stayed at the beach longer than we should have. We all still needed to go to our hotel and check in as well as dress up for our dinner spot. We had a reservation in the little Italy section of San Diego. This area was a little older and more upper-class environment than we were used to. We were only a couple years removed from college. While we all had grown up jobs, we really were not out of the flow of our college years. It was our time to explore with absolute reckless abandon. Ok, maybe it was just the guys who were on the reckless side.

George had booked our hotel with all his special Marriott points he accumulated through his job. Ava and I could not complain about the stay. It was going to cost us a dinner and drinks. Absolutely fair trade. Even though it was San Diego, it was not downtown, and it was not near the beach. It was one of the Marriott's they conveniently forgot to up-grade. It was a few decades old. It also had one room and a tiny bathroom.

My poor wife. Poor is a key word there. While we all had grown up jobs, we all had the usual student loan debt, and other debts that came with adulting. When we did our trips, we had to cut corners some-where. It was never eating, drinking, or shopping. We seemed to always cut the cost in the sleeping arrangements. It also ended up with my wife being the only girl in the room. Not ideal, but we always seemed to manage. We generally partied the night away in any locale and only utilized the room for a short amount of time to sleep and get ready. We rarely spent any time in our room. This was also the early 2000's, be-fore smartphones were invented, and there was no Air BNB or Hotels. com to comparison shop. You got what you got. George got us this two full size beds and bathroom bungalow for the price of a dinner and a bottle of wine. It was a steal.

WRECKLESSLY ABSURD

Frank bought a twelve pack of Stroh's beer, so we had something to drink while we got ready. While we patiently waited on my wife to beautify, the three of us continued the drinking. George and I should have probably stopped when we got to the hotel and took a power nap. Frank could drink his ass off when it came to beer. Hard alcohol was different. George was a heavy-set Ewok, but he could always drink two beers to Frank and I's one. I was also limited on my lack of body mass. Back then, Frank had me by 200 plus pounds and George had me by about 150. Trying to keep up with them in drinking was always a mistake. I do like a good challenge though.

I barely remember the ride to dinner. At least it was a 20-minute ride with some fresh air blowing in our faces. That helped the three guys at least wake up. Ava was just happy to have her good friend there. It would also be for her to balance out some of the testosterone with some estrogen.

When we got to the restaurant, we found out we beat Barb. Our wait on a table was short as Barb had already made reservations for our party. The hostess escorted us out to the veranda and our table for six. Which was odd. It should only have been five of us. Maybe they had just miscounted. George immediately ordered a bottle of fine wine and a heaping order of jumbo cocktail shrimp. These were a standard go to for George at every nice dinner. I never could figure out why he loved jumbo cock so much.

We were all well into the wine and stupid jokes when my wife perked up. She had set her eyes on her relief for the night: Barb had entered the building. We also saw why the table count was at six. Barb had a new man. Or at least a new date for the night. Our group generally runs with the motto: the more the merrier. This was one of those nights.

We all hugged Barb and said our hellos. Barb then introduced us to Chandler, her new boyfriend. Ava was her usual charming self and welcomed them both and immediately got into catching up with Barb. Which left poor Chandler to deal with three drunk strange dudes. I am not 100% sure that his name was Chandler. I think he reminded me of Chandler from the hit TV show Friends.

This poor guy had unwittingly walked into the lion's den. George and I should apologize to Chandler. We were young and stupid, and Chandler happened to be dating the girl that broke our good friend, Murray's, heart. George and I thought Barb could have been "the one" for Murray. When their relationship went south a couple years prior, we saw Murray become "that single guy" for life. George and I are idiots. We were not in tune with the fact that Murray was not heart broken, nor did he ever want to seriously date anyone ever again. Single life suited Murray like bling on a rapper.

The three guys gave Chandler a limp handshake and a lame welcome to the party. This guy was an officer in the Navy, just like Murray. This guy was even an engineer working in the nuclear subs. Just like Murray. It was all so very Twilight Zone. Had Barb found an exact replica of our good friend?

George and I could see Frank was losing his shit. Franks side glances and googly eyes, he was making indicated that he too found this situation very odd. I should probably mention that Ava had a tight grip on my leg and was giving me some gentle kicks under the table. She saw the stupid looks the three of us were giving each other. She also knew how drunk we already were and how uninhibited we got at that stage.

For the most part we did keep it civil. My wife took charge of the conversation as much as she could. She wanted to genuinely catch up with her friend whom she hadn't seen since our wedding a couple years ago. Which left Mr. Bing alone with the smartass lions. The one thing that was different with him than our buddy Murray was that Chandler was not much of a talker. Nor was he much of an outgoing person. I guess to be fair he was surrounded by a bunch of drunk guys who he had never met before.

The three of us thought we were so undercover funny, and we started to pepper in small Murray name drops into the dinner conversation. Frank, who was usually the lead in most of the hi-jinx situations like this, was behaving himself. He probably saw my wife's sideways glances and death-clutch on my leg and decided to keep it together. George and I were starting to get out of control.

As soon as we had ordered our dinner George mentioned that he had to use the bathroom. Chandler and Barb were now painfully aware of our childish humor and pettiness. Barb explained to her new boyfriend that we were all friends with her previous boyfriend. Chandler played it off cool; he understood the situation with everyone at the table. Barb was also smart enough to have had that conversation with Chandler before dinner. Just in case it came up. George and I started to push our childish humor and it started to become mean natured. Ava told me to go refresh myself and take a quick timeout. I knew the look she gave me. I got up and followed George out of the restaurant.

George and I stumbled our way out the back patio. It was one of those small open-air malls with odd and ends type of retail stores attached. The bathroom was shared by these businesses, so it meant we had to navigate around half a mile of these random shops. We slowly made our way to the commode. We were making each other laugh with our stupid jokes. We both noticed a gift shop with a ton of souvenir and touristy type gifts that was right next to the bathroom.

What happened next is still in contention, but I will tell you my recollection. Sometime during the bathroom stop, an idea was born. It was a horrible idea, but an idea, nonetheless. George decided that it would be funny to stop by the gift shop and look for something hilarious that we could bring back to the dinner table. We would get Frank to burst out in laughter and come over to the dark side with us.

We finished up our business and walked into the gift shop. It is important to note that this usual five-minute pee trip had already tripled in time frame. Jokes, looking at shops, and getting lost, had all added to the overall time of this little jaunt. Probably best for the dinner party, or so George and I thought.

It took us about another 15 minutes of looking around to finally figure out that we couldn't find the right joke. We needed to get back to dinner as Chandler and Frank were probably stealing our wine. Our food might even be there by now. Just as we are leaving, the nice owner summoned us over. She told us she noticed us walk by and then come back in. She wanted to know if she could direct us to what we were looking for, even if it was not in her store. Awesome customer service, and if there is anything that George is a sucker for, it's grade A customer service. Just ask his repo guy, Chris.

We told her about our current plight. She looked bewildered at our nonsensical story. Yet she somehow knew exactly what we needed. She pointed over to a small rack that we both had walked past. Indeed, she was unquestionably correct. It was like she was a god and she was literally shining a direct light on our answer. We took a couple of minutes to browse through the selection of items. The problem we had was that there was no proper way to display these two items that we wanted to buy.

This lovely old lady would not let us go in defeat. She said she knew a way that we could display these items, but it would take a few minutes. George and I looked at each other with hope, and decided since we had only been gone about seven minutes (in our mathematical estimation), what was another three or so?

My wife will someday confirm the facts of this story, but here is what probably took place. About 45 minutes after George and I's little hike to the bathroom we finally stumbled victoriously through the palm trees to our dinner party. Not only had our dinner come, but the other four were already halfway through their main course and a couple bottles of wine.

Their eyes pretty much told George and I everything we needed to know. My wife's eyes were ice cold. Barb's eyes were evenly matched with a tinge of utter shock. Chandler's eyes were a mix of confusion plus that sad look like when you put down your pet. Frank's eyes were a solid mix of what the fuck did you two assholes just do and a partial evil recognition of what we just did topped with utter sorrow for what was about to follow.

George and I knew it was time to sit down. Our brand new shiny mini-license plate name tags were perfectly lit by our tables lamp. They were bouncing around our necks with the homemade rubber band necklace the lovely shop owner took time to make. What really stood out were the names that were on each license plate.

I took the high road. I decided that it would be funny if I came back to the table with Frank's old girlfriend first name, Ashley. She and Frank had a tumultuous relationship from the get-go, but they had been giving it their best and she had even moved to LA with him right after college. People have different motivations and wants in life. People break up, get divorced, and move on. Frank and Ashley had just broken up and he was only starting to feel out the new options in his life.

While I thought I was trying to be funny, I also felt I was really help-ing Frank. He needed to get over any of his "break up blues" he might still have. Helping with laughter, it's my motto in life. However, laugh-ter is very subjective to taste and personal interpretation. Frank was not amused. Nor was anyone else at the table, especially my wife. The hatred heat wave she was throwing my way was inescapable.

George unfortunately jumped on the proverbial hand grenade and took the super low road. His license plate just happened to have Barb's former boy toy, and our good friend's name on it. Murray was even spelled correctly. Safe to say that George and I tied for the worst deci-sion ever made that night. Our hilariously awesome joke that took us over forty minutes to concoct, did not get two thumbs up from Roger or Ebert. There would have probably been eight thumbs, all pointing down.

Dinner was deathly quiet and painfully slow for the next half hour.

As soon as Barb and Mr. Bing were done, they promptly paid their bill and said their short goodbyes. My wife gave them the "I am so sorry" look and the "don't blame me" hugs. Barb and Chandler gave her the "We feel so sorry for you! We get to leave but you are stuck with this lot!" look. Girls are spectacular at communicating with looks and body motions only.

The anger that poured out of my wife was unfathomable. As angry as she was at George, she was double if not triple as angry with me. Frank quickly came to her side and immediately laid into us. He asked us where the hell we disappeared to for the last hour. I corrected him and said it was really 45 minutes. No laughter. Tough crowd.

It was all starting to come into focus for us now. George and I started telling them the exact same path that I explained above. Frank and my wife did not find this blueprint for disaster as amusing as George and I did. Frank did show a slightly hidden smile of understanding, but since this was a rare "it's not me this time" moment for himself, he was going to at least have some fun with it. Ava? Not so much.

Ava stormed off. As I ran after her I could faintly hear George mutter out loud that we were just having a little fun. No ill will was ever intended. Frank slugged him, told him that they needed to go get a beer and leave Ava and I alone to calmly discuss the issues at hand. As with most couple fights, I think we all wish that was really what happened. Not this time.

I vaguely recall the one-sided verbal sparring match that happened as I caught up with Ava. I remember that 90% of the time she was using choice words and trying to understand my mentality. I successfully defended myself about 1% of the time. That fateful night, my two future children, almost did not happen. Somehow, by the grace of Amphictyonies, I convinced my wife to not divorce me. I swore George and I would apologize to Barb and Chandler for our childish behavior. She wasn't mad that we were trying to lighten the mood, she was just mad we picked a poor time and place to do such an idiotic thing.

The agreement to not disagree between Ava and I took about the same amount of time it took for George and me to ruin the nice dinner and evening out. Frank and George were watching us from the protection of bar inside the restaurant. Frank needed more alcohol to help to erase the memory of what just occurred. George was trying to guesstimate his window of opportunity to profusely apologize to Ava. When they saw us hug and kiss, they knew it was time to call it a night. It was already past 1 AM.

As George was saying sorry to my wife, I just stumbled along, minding my P's and Q's. When we finally got back to our little hotel room, we were almost all back to normal. My wife was at least smiling and might have laughed once. Frank was in heaven as he was finally able to make fun of George and I and there was not a damn thing we could do about it. We all agreed that a late-night pizza was in order. Our dinner was not that great and not many people ended up eating. This small gesture also made Ava happy.

When we got inside our tiny room, we let my wife make the call for food. She could order whatever she wanted, and we gave her our order as well. She was the smartest one in that room and no mistakes would be made. The problem was she was too nice and listened to what the three drunk bozos wanted to eat. Once she knew food was on the way, she went to the bathroom to clean up and get ready for bed.

Frank, George, and I somehow reverted to the fourth-grade sleepover mentality. You know, the one where you get to have a sleepover with your buddies and get to stay up super late? We also thought that it should also turn into WWE wrestling match. Which was dumb on my part. Not only did Frank have a good 200 pounds on me, but George was an ex middle school wrestling stand out. His name is probably still on the Marauders hall of fame. Did not stop my 150-pound body from entering the dome.

Where the night decidedly took the worst turn was when my wife emerged from the bathroom about 30 minutes later. She heard some-one pounding on our hotel door. She came out of the bathroom wanting to know why one of us was not answering the door. She regrettably was greeted with that answer. When she looked to the right towards the two full sized beds, she saw the three of us passed out. We were all in one bed. What was strange to her was that we all had our shirts off, and for some odd reason George had his pants off as well. He was naked except for his "Ken Crawfish" branded tighty whiteys.

Someday Ava can tell her side of this story. I sure it will be a delight for all.

As she slowly opened the door, I assume she made the pizza delivery guy blush. He had to wonder why this petite woman was paying for four large pizzas all for herself. He then got a good scan of the room and saw something straight out of a porno that no one wanted to watch. Three of the sexiest guys, all in a state of undress, and passed out with each other in one bed. At least Ava got one of the beds to herself with no one to bother her. She could get the glorious sleep she so deserved.

That was true until George started snoring at his usual 15 decibel volume. Even better for Ava was that Frank and I joined in with George's mutant snoring sounds. The three tenors, as my wife would always say. It was not her favorite weekend.

Square Danced into My Heart

I will be the first to admit that I love a great prank. Whether it is physical in nature or simply to mess with someone's head. I just think we all need a little laughter in our lives because most of us have become way too intense and cynical in our adult lives. I like to make fun out of molehills. I never intend to hurt anyone with my pranks or jokes. I simply want to make people laugh.

Sometimes my pranks required extensive planning and involved many people. This can be very delicate. I advise you to be very, very careful, especially when involving your parents. Specifically, your mother. You better make sure that the prank is innocent and will not completely embarrass her. Your dad? That's your call and your life. Live it how you want to.

This particular prank I played was the long con. One that took a lot of time to set up and to fully allow to come to fruition. In fact, the set up was so long, I honestly forgot I even put the prank in motion until a couple weeks before it all played out. My poor wife, Ava. To be fair to her, she was the one that decided married me.

My mother is a wonderful soul. She can also be cantankerous and opinionated. But unlike my father, she succumbs to facts and will admit when she is wrong. However, she is hardly ever wrong. In fact, she literally used to be my own personal Siri, before Siri was a thing. She hated, but secretly loved, that non-paying job. Random Saturday morning calls at 3:30 AM from her youngest child, only to be asked some trivial fact about historical characters or personal experiences to settle a bet with someone. Don't worry, I always apologize for the late call. My mother is also be very persistent when she wants an answer to her own questions. Not answering is not an option. She will continue to ask until she finally gets an answer. It was best to provide some response, even if that response is not remotely close to correct.

My mom loves my wife, more than me honestly, and I don't blame her. Ava is great. My mom is a planner and like things done far in advance if possible. It was early April and we were back in Montana for some reason and my mom took me aside and in a serious tone asked me what I thought Ava would like for Christmas. It was sweet and heartfelt. She wanted to have plenty of time to find a gift or do something special for Ava for next Christmas when we would be back home. I hoped eight months of planning would be enough time for her.

Her question awoke that devious 1% of my brain. I had already told my mom that I had no clue this early. We knew each other well enough, but we were still young and impressionable, and this was the start of the 2000s. Everything was changing quickly these days, especially our tastes and wants. But my mom would not take "no" for an answer. She was dead set on knowing early because she had something in mind. I still am not sure where my brain went on this one, but I just rolled with it and told my mom that Ava had always been into square dancing. I also told her that she had been the state champion back in her high school days in Wyoming, with a couple of titles. To be clear, my wife probably danced a square dance with me once, back at our wedding reception. Never before or after that with any regularity. With my mom satisfied and barely even questioning my answer, I was able to get back to whatever it was I was up to. I also conveniently forgot to tell my mom I was only kidding. I really did forget I told her that little white lie . . . until about seven months later when my mom randomly told me something over the phone.

When I called my mom that weekend in November, it was simply to let her know we had purchased our plane tickets to fly home for Christmas. She was delighted. I know what a big deal it was for all her kids to be home for the holidays, but she was another level of happy. I quickly found out why: she excitedly told me how proud she was of the gift that she had commissioned for my wife. I had to double check that I had heard her correctly.

When I asked my mom to clarify what she was so giddy about, she almost didn't tell me. She wanted it to be a surprise to me as well. After a little prodding, my mom finally agreed that it would be OK to tell me. She had paid one of her sisters, who did a lot of sewing and quilt work, to make a special piece of clothing for my wife. When she told me that my aunt had completed the piece, a little bit of my memory recalled a random question my mom had asked many months before. She told me that she had a traditional square dance outfit handmade for Ava. By my Aunt. It was fit for a champion.

I had a couple of choices and an absolute at this point. The absolute thing was that I had to bite my finger and move my mouth away from the phone so as not to alert my mother to the extreme suppression of uncontrollable laughter that was soon to overtake my body. I managed to succeed.

The next two choices were critical to the success of the long con. I could tell my mom that I was, in fact, joking when I told her that Ava was a championship square dancer. I had kind of half expected that she had already figured that out. However, if I told her the truth right there, she would be a little sad that her kind thoughts and over the top execution would be for naught. Then I had the second option: tell her that Ava would be so happy and excited as she loved my mom and would appreciate the extra thought and work that went into getting such a unique and wonderful gift. I sided with option two. I felt that it would have the maximum humor for all involved and make our general festive Christmas Eve family get together even more memorable. I was coming off a disastrous first Christmas with my wife and my family. Not for them, but for me. That story from my previous book helped strengthen the bond between my parents, my sisters, and Ava. By our second Christmas together, things could only be better.

I held that little nugget in the back of my head and tried my hardest to not think about it. However, there would be mornings where Ava would tell me that I woke her up the previous night by laughing out loud. She said it kind of creeped her out as she just shook me, and I went back to sleep. I had a bad poker face in my REM state apparently. I played it off as one of my many interactive and over imaginative dreams.

Christmas finally arrived. Ava and I were always excited to go back to where we met. We still had a good number of friends and family in Missoula and it was always busy and brutally fucking cold. But always an awesome little vacation.

We flew in a few days before Christmas, so Ava and my mom had plenty of time to hang out. I did love that my wife had taken to my crazy family. Relationships with in-laws can make or break marriages. We both lucked out as we both loved our respective set of in-laws. Both families loved to get together with talk about anything and everything under the sun. Always with a copious amount of wine or almond champagne, and a smorgasbord of delicious food.

It was inevitable that my mom would attempt to throw out her own inside jokes and make random comments about country music and square dancing. Ava did not bite. She had no idea why my mom was talking about country music. She figured it was something she just missed in between glasses of champagne. I, on the other hand, was quite amused with all the interactions I overheard. I then went back to playing World Wrestling Federation Royal Rumble with all my young nieces and nephews, a Christmas Eve tradition that I made up. All those kids will tell you the reason they have all gone on to such successful careers is because of the amount of pile drivers their awesome uncle Chance gave them.

The Christmas Eve festivities were wrapping. It was time for my siblings to move onto their own houses and the guests had mainly come and gone. My mom had a public announcement before anyone could leave. She needed everyone to open their Christmas Eve gift from my dad and her. Each kid and each grandkid got to open one gift of my mom's choosing before they left for the night. It was a tradition that made no sense, but that I still adore and keep going to this very day. Ava was not used to it as her family never had that tradition. That is the awesome thing about her, she just goes with the flow. I was really banking on that great attitude and the amount of booze that was consumed that night to really help with my mother's surprise gift to my wife.

My nieces and nephews opened the requisite toys and special things they asked for. My mom made gift giving an absolute art. Sometimes it was as simple as giving what they asked for; other times, like this one for my wife, it was a more thoughtfully planned gift. I can't remember what my sisters got but I'm sure it was nice clothing. Probably Ralph Lauren My mom was in a phase of getting that brand for everyone. It was also one of Ava's favorite clothing brands during that time period as well. I think I got some college gear or something like that. All the other gifts were a blur as I was only focused on the finale, Ava's gift.

This is the part where I confess. The guilt that built up inside me about not letting my Mom know about my misguided information about Ava was eating me up. The night we had arrived in Missoula, I pulled my mom aside and told her I had to tell her something. She took that the wrong way and thought I was about to tell her that Ava was pregnant, which made my predicament even more challenging. Now I had to tell her that, no, we were not even close. We were having no discussions about babies. I had, however, told her a little white lie. I broke the unfortunate news that my wife was not a square dance title holder, and in fact she had never even square danced once.

When my mom slapped my arm and called me an asshole, it was totally expected. It was when she started laughing that I was caught off guard. I asked her why she was laughing, or was she crying? She informed me that she was laughing because even though I was a jerk to do that to Ava and her, she saw something great coming out of this whole surprise. She said she absolutely was going to still give Ava the dress, but now it would have more sentimental meaning for both of them and a moment they would share forever. Plus, there was no way my mom was telling her sister that she just put all that effort into the dress, and it was for naught.

My mom's smile was as wide as I have ever seen on that snowy Christmas Eve night. My wife had a huge box in front of her. In fact, it was the largest gift box given that night. My wife's smile and excitement were only second to my mother's. My little nieces and nephews were transfixed on the spectacle because they knew the bigger the gift box, usually the better the present. My sisters and their significant others had stopped chatting to focus on mom's special surprise gift. They were happy this gift was not coming from me.

As my wife gently tore apart the wrapping, my mom blurted out, "Oh Ava, just rip it all apart! I won't save any of that wrapping paper or ribbons." That was all Ava needed to rip the rest of the paper off to reveal only a generic brown moving box. As she grabbed a knife to cut open the box, she was telling me that my mom went too far. This seemed like too much of a gift. I assured her with a muffled laugh to just wait for the final product.

I still have the picture progression as she opened the box to see what looked like a beautiful and very ornate dress. Which is somewhat impressive because I was using a camera with actual film. The shade of pure white to pure red that Ava's face displayed within three pictures was perfect. As she opened the gift, she was perplexed. She lifted this sunlight yellow dress with layers of white ruffles. She was embarrassed because she knew this was important to my mom but had no idea what she was holding. It was not a normal dress she could wear in the classroom.

When she looked over to me and saw me doubled over with laughter, her red turned a little more towards the angry shade. She knew something was afoot. The rest of the family was just as perplexed as Ava. My nephews were sad it wasn't a new gaming system and my nieces were "oohing and awing" over the beauty of this dress. It was a real princess dress. Thankfully, my mom broke the silence.

She told Ava that this was a traditional square-dancing dress from years ago. She explained that my aunt had used her old square-dancing dress design to sew this one together from scratch. My wife, still not in on the joke, played it off perfectly. She said it was beautiful and was obviously hand crafted. But she had one question: what made my mom think to get her this specific dress?

"Well, my asshole son decided to lie to me and told me almost a year ago that you were a championship square dancer and that you take him out every other weekend to square dance events," My mom happily shouted out to the family.

Ava calmly turned to address the entire family and let them know that not only was she not a square dancer, but she wouldn't even know a square-dancing dress if she saw one, which she was holding in her hands. The entire family broke down laughing. Not laughing at my wife, but just the amount of effort and time into this prank.

My mom came over and hugged my wife and explained it all. My wife could do nothing but grab another glass of wine and laugh with everyone.

Later when we were headed to bed, she was still laughing about the whole thing. No bad blood or ill will. She did wonder out loud what goes through my head when I come up with half the shit that comes out of my mouth. It was then that another older memory sparked in my head.

"Oh shit," I thought. I remembered that I told someone, who I could not remember, that my wife was a semi-pro bowler. I tried my hardest to remember who that was. I would remember in the morning and correct that another white lie. Maybe it was my brother or a good friend. I just smiled at my wife and let her know that I just loved her so much that I liked to always keep everything in our relationship fun and spontaneous. With that we kissed and passed out to get ready for Christmas Day.

Spoiler alert: I finally found out who I told about that bowling tidbit. It was my mom.

WHEN THE WALLS COME TUMBLIN' DOWN

I have been dedicated to music my entire life. Music has shaped me, comforted me, and gave me extra motivation in different facets throughout my life. I even put music lyrics at the start of every chapter of my previous book as an homage to bands I loved. I also used a line or lines from a song that would generally fit into the story the reader was about to embark on. Music will always be coursing through my veins.

I really missed my calling to somehow be involved with that love of mine. I guess that's why I am now making a splash with my books so I can become the next Hank Moody, writing incredible autobiographies and memoirs of some of the biggest musical stars out there. Nothing wrong with a dream and a plan.

Life for me was about as crazy as it could get. I was working nonstop hours with a major corporation, hustling for any extra dollars. Ava and I had our first little monster and that new lifestyle was taking up more time than either of us ever anticipated. Our second incoming monster was still a year away. My wife was in as great spirits. Especially since this was a very tumultuous time in our lives.

When I picked up the phone thinking I was getting into a routine business call, I was pleasantly surprised. It was indeed a business client, but also someone that had turned into a good friend. He had some concert tickets that he had intended to use, but something had come up. He wanted to know if I could use them. It was for the Snoop Dogg after party. Snoop a Loop was playing as the headliner at the 420 festival up at Red Rocks amphitheater. On Easter. That was Snoop's day gig. His night gig had turned into being a professional DJ. Which is the concert I was being offered. Calvin would have some of his up and coming rappers open for him and then he would come out and DJ the rest of the concert It was an interesting concept and makes perfect sense in the realm of Snoop. I immediately told my buddy to email me the tickets. They would get used.

It was a Sunday night and my wife had to be up early the next day for her job. She was out on going to the free hookup. I started looking at my little black book and calling on people who might be interested and who I knew were probably in town. Almost everyone had something going on already or just had no interest. It was then that I remembered my good old buddy, Glen Dwyer. I considered him first as he was always down for some random fun, but he traveled so much I just assumed he was out of town. When I sent him over a text, I fully expected to not to hear from him. He was probably in Germany securing new financing for his next shadow company. I was in luck. My phone started ringing and sure as shit, it was Glen.

Glen was a longtime friend. I have known him since High School. He wasn't the best "go with the flow" type of personality. He always had to know the times of events and double check all facts within a given opportunity. He always had to weigh the odds. This time though, he simply wanted to know what time I would be picking him up and if he had time to change clothes. This was a new and improved Glen. I loved to see this side of him. I told him I would see him in about thirty minutes or so. He had plenty of time. I had to finish up Easter stuff with the wife and kiddo and get changed myself.

When the Uber driver picked me up, I had to laugh. My economy Uber was a four seat, 1990 Toyota Corolla. It was also being driven by a much larger lady and I could hear Bob Marley playing on the car stereo. At least her car was very super clean, and she was very pleasant. We had a very short drive to Glen's house to pick him up. It was enough time for the nice Uber driver and I to share a pleasant conversation. She was excited to hear we were going to see Snoop late night. He was one of her favorite rappers growing up.

When we got to Glen's place, I sent him a text to let him know we were out front waiting for him. He said he would be out in a minute. No rush or hurry I texted back to him. We would get to the venue early as is. We were going to do a little pre-partying prior to the concert. Both of us had very easy Monday mornings, so we could afford to get a little tipsier that night. We also both finished our Easter duties with our respective families and were off the leash at that point.

When Glen walked out of his house there was a distinct vibe to his walk. I had seen that before, so it was with no surprise that when he opened the door the waft of aged whiskey hit myself and the Uber driver like a brick. When I asked him what party he had been attending all day he informed me that he had family over earlier and had to self-medicate to get through it. He was so happy to see my text as he wanted to continue his party, but he needed a break from the family. Plus, it was Snoop fucking Dogg. He couldn't pass on that grass.

Glen had a tumultuous history with cab drivers. Sometimes it could be uncomfortable to be in the same car with him when it was a stranger driving. The weird thing was that he had a limo driver that he employed. The only reason we were in an Uber that night and not using his driver was that his driver was out of town. When Glen rolled out a couple of very inappropriate jokes for the entire car to hear all I could do was bury my face in my hands. Our Uber driver did not find his inappropriate jokes and comments very funny. The next 20 minutes to the concert venue was very quiet. Now and again I would try to break the silence, but it would just turn into some unintelligible mumbles from Glen and then him laughing at his own jokes.

As the Uber driver happily dropped us off at the front of the concert venue, I let Glen get out ahead of me. I quietly gave the nice lady a 20 spot and without even saying a word our eyes locked and I tried to communicate it was harmless inappropriateness from my buddy and no harm no foul. She took the money and ran.

I followed Glen to the front of the concert hall. I noticed he had already stumbled up to the front ticket window. The employee there told us that Snoop's Easter 420 concert went long. He and his other acts would be starting a little late tonight. Glen was so happy. Now we had time to find the nearest watering hole and really get after it. The party before the party was what Glen was all about.

We quickly ran into our first problem. This area of Denver was going through a kind of gentrification process. Colorado was still a few years from legalizing marijuana and this part of town had not been part of the revitalization plan. There were only a few businesses in the area. Most of the building were boarded up. The huge hospital and this old concert venue were the only things to note in the immediate vicinity. That didn't deter Glen or his mission. He already had his phone out and was looking up the nearest bar. Sure, enough there was one within three blocks. Off we went. We figured we had about an hour before we needed to be back to the venue.

When we got to where this bar was supposed to be, we both just had to stop and look at each other. His phone had led us to the parking lot of this run-down motel. You know, the stereotypical hourly rate motel with three or four old jalopies parked out front. I asked Glen if he was sure that this was the place. He looked over the info again and the interweb said this mythical place was open. It also had an amazing 2 out of 5-star Yelp review. We started heading towards the front desk area of the motel to ask someone that worked there if they could direct us. We walked right past this huge red door to the side of this motel. This red door had a distinct neon "open" sign. We had found our dive bar.

We walked in and were greeted with the foul smell of years old puke and stale beer. We also saw a 70-year-old grandma behind the bar. She was shaking her head at the sight of us. We were not her typical regulars and she knew right away that we were out of our element. Nothing was going to get between Glen and his next round of whiskey.

Two Fireball shots and a triple Jack and Coke on the rocks later, we found ourselves in a lively conversation with the old timers that were crowded around the bar. They wanted to know how the hell we stumbled on this little motel bar. We explained we were just waiting on a concert a few blocks away. When we told them we were seeing Snoop, the bartender bought us a couple more Fireball shots. She said we were going to need it as we were probably going to be the only two old dudes at that concert. We laughed it off but absolutely appreciated the free round. I was way behind Glen in the booze intake, but I was at least feeling that whiskey warmth roll through my body. We chugged down our last beer before closing out and heading back to the venue.

When we started down the block towards the Gothic Theater, I could sense something was off. Glen was walking just fine and still speaking well, but his eyes and cheeks were something else. It was a cool night for Denver, especially this late into April. Enough that we knew to bring our coats along. Glen's cheeks were flushed red that one could mistake were due to that cold night. I knew better. His eyes could only be described as cloudy ice. He was more hammered than when I picked him up. I knew Glen well enough to have seen this state of inebriation before.

I told him to slow down a little. He said he was great and then jumped on my back like we were 12 years old again. His behavior was a little off, but I was in a lightened mood, so I just went with it. We still had a six block walk back to the venue, so that would help sober him up a tiny bit.

We finally made it to the Gothic Theater and gave them our free VIP tickets. VIP was a stretch. Our seats were bar stools with backs. At least we were almost center stage. We also had a tiny table for any food or drink. Better than standing for the whole performance. Glen could use a few minutes in his seat to get his wits about him.

We were sitting down by the new time the concert was to start. Sure enough one of the promoters came out and announced that Snoop was on his way but had some traffic and he was going to be a little later than the audience was last told. The venue was not full by any means; the Gothic held around a thousand people at most but there was probably a third of that amount. We had purchased a round of drinks before we got to our seats as we did not know we still had a bunch of time.

Glen was on fire that night. In the couple of minutes it took for us to get to our table Glen had already almost downed his Jack and Coke. I took a seat, taking in the crowd. I couldn't help but to laugh at how correct the prior bar manager's prediction was. Glen smacked my back, almost knocking me off my stool. He told me that he needed to go to the bathroom and that he would grab another round for us. He would be right back.

I noticed that more people were filing in. It looked like Snoops pre-party posse had made it before their headliner. The show would be starting soon. Which then reminded me, where the fuck did Glen go? The place was still only about half full. I assumed he had to take a longer bathroom break than expected. I guess he could also be jammed up in a bar line.

I was enjoying the pre-party music as well as talking to the concert goers seated around us. They announced the first act, rapper YG, would be on stage soon. I was starting to wonder if Glen had bounced. He had a history of doing that. It was this internal self-defense mechanism that he had. There are so many instances in my history that I wish my brain had that instinct.

The concert was now officially about to start. YG's posse were on stage and shouting out some very California specific things. Funny enough, nothing about the resurrection of Christ ever came up in those hype rantings. I was getting my cell out of my pocket to call Glen when suddenly I felt about 190 pounds crash into me. There he was, right in the nick of time. My drink had just run out.

Glen did not come back bearing alcoholic gifts though. Right after he smashed into me, he took his seat the best he could. His glossed-out eyes were void of consciousness. When he realized I was staring at him with questioning wonder his brain sparked enough willpower to tell me where he was for the past 30 minutes. He didn't need to say a word. I saw that Glen had two giant X's in permanent black sharpie ink on his hands. They were so large, that even with the lack of lights in our section, they were unmistakable.

He was utterly bombed at this point. I only knew it because his "tell" sign was his huge grin. The slurred speech was also a dead giveaway. He garbled something about the bouncers were being utter assholes. I knew his line of bullshit when I heard it. It was not my first rodeo with Glen. Right then those asshole bouncers showed up right behind Glen. My suspicions were confirmed.

They grabbed Glen to steady him, so he didn't fall off his stool. They then let me know that they had given Glen the big double X's because he was now banned from ordering anymore alcohol. They also said that if they caught him violating these conditions, they had no choice but to ask him to leave the premises. Given the build up to the night I figured these blokes had their wits about themselves and were spot on with assessing Glen's behavior. I apologized to them and assured them that he would be fine, and no more alcohol would be coming his way.

As soon as the bouncers left, Glen made one of the smartest choices ever. He was done for. He wanted to get an Uber and go home. Generally, I would be pissed about someone leaving me by myself at an event I invited them to. But the crowd was fun, and the tickets were a free. I was not about to try to argue for Glen to stay. He was a wreck and fading fast. It had been a long two hours since I picked him up at his place.

I helped him navigate his Uber app to get his ride. It was a chore. The good news was that his Uber driver was right around the corner. I could easily help Glen out the front door and still get back into the venue just in time to catch the first act.

What happened next will always remain in the realm of mystery. I will tell my version of the story. I walked Glen out the front door. With both bouncers right behind us I walked him within 15 feet of his Uber. I let him go and told him that I was heading back into the theater to watch the show start and that I would catch up with him soon enough. When I looked back before reentering the venue, I saw that he was literally 10 steps away from his Uber.

When I came back in the bouncers thanked me for taking care of the situation as they were probably going to have to tell him he had to go anyhow. I thanked them back for letting me know and went back to my table.

The concert was just starting. I ended up making it through the opener and a majority of Snoop. Sadly, Snoop was a little more into his DJ career at that time and wasn't doing any rapping. He was letting the newbies get their moment. Good stuff, but I was without my buddy and getting a little too buzzed. So about two hours after the concert started, I decided to call it quits. I got my Uber and took the 20-minute ride home. I noticed there was some activity on my phone, but I was not paying that much attention to it. My wife knew I was on my way home and that's all I needed to worry about.

The next morning when I saw a flurry of missed text notifications from multiple different people that I figured something was going on. The very first text I got was from a mutual friend that Glen and both knew. That friend was going to come to the concert with us but I think he was wrapped up with family stuff so he couldn't make it. His initial text was a bit confusing. He was letting me know that I should have stayed out with Glen. Glen apparently did not end his night as I thought he did. Confused, I simply texted our friend back that I had zero clue what he was talking about. I even told him I put Glen in his Uber and he should have been to go. Nope. Not the case.

Our mutual buddy then sent me a text picture of Glen. I am looking at that picture right now and still do not have the right words to do this picture justice. I will try though. There was my buddy Glen, in some sort of ER room, lying on an emergency room cot. He has that same huge drunk grin he had displayed the prior night. He was wearing the same clothes even. But he was now sporting a full neck brace, and his face was scraped up and there is dried blood on him and his clothes.

Stunned, I sent our mutual buddy, Jeff, back a text message. The subject matter was simple and to the point. "What the actual fuck?" I was so bamboozled at this picture of Glen and the turn of events that I was at a loss for words. Jeff could not get the whole story from Glen. He was only able to glean a little bit of info from his wife. It was also then that I noticed the activity from the previous night included a missed call and text from Jeff. I just only seeing it all now. The puzzle was slowly starting to be put together

From the info that Jeff got, Glen had told his wife that I had never stepped outside the Gothic with him. He said he had stumbled outside and then magically woke up in a hospital, 4 hours later. I am not going to call bullshit on the poor guy, but I will at least defend myself and say that I did enough that should have gotten him home safely. The only other thing I could have done is to have taken those final ten steps and literally put him in the back seat of the Uber.

The problem in this story is that Glen was so out of it, and whatever happened to him impacted his frontal lobe so much, that his acute memory of what really happened will be hidden forever. Only the JFK murder plot could match the conspiracy he was telling his wife. He was not telling anyone what really happened. Jeff said there was an official police report. But Glen and his wife were not divulging those details.

I have a few theories though. These are only my guess's. I just looked at Glens prior history and previously known facts. With that said let's break down the possible scenarios.

My guess is that between those 10 steps to the Uber he had some sort of relapse. Which type of relapse? A few options are available.

Theory #1: He could have tussled with different folks outside the venue for his Uber and he could have lost that tussle. Resulting in hitting his head or his entire face on the sidewalk. Which then resulted in someone calling for an ambulance and thus ending up in the ER room of Swedish General. Somehow, he gave Jeff's number so that he could come pick him up while being as discreet as possible.

Theory #2: He made it to the Uber. He decided that the dumb bouncers were wrong. He would show them all. So, he decides to go back to the same dive bar we had left earlier. While at that bar he got even more trashed which somehow resulted in his intake to said ER room at said hospital. Or he possibly said the wrong thing to someone at this bar and got into a one-sided fight which also resulted with him in the infirmary.

Theory #3: He got into the Uber and then lost all brain functions. His system malfunctioned thus leading him to revert to his old cabbie abusing self. He got verbally abusive with his driver. His driver did not take kindly to Glen's verbal assault. Words were exchanged, the driver pulled over. Then the driver dragged Glen out of the backseat and beat the hell him. The Uber driver then sped off leaving Glen in a puddle of blood on the side of the street. Glen stayed there until a kind Samaritan found him and called an ambulance. This theory is a stretch, but it should be noted that Glen had a previous altercation with a cabby a few years prior that ended up just like above.

To this day, Glen still claims he has little memory of that night. He tried to lay the blame on me. Which I will accept a portion of that blame. I was the reason he went to the concert that fateful evening. Granted we were both adults and he by no means had to say yes. Especially since he had obviously been hitting bottle a little too much that day before I even got to him. I will also accept the fact I did put him into the Uber's back seat. But damn Glen, you had like ten fucking steps to get to safety.

Maybe someday I will get to see the official police report that only Glen and his wife saw. To be fair I am not even sure his wife has seen that report. I was just told she had. Either way, Glen is still rocking in the free world and marching to the beat of his own drum. He even broke his own rule and came to a concert with me in late 2018. Jeff was even in attendance with us at that same Missio concert. I am happy to report that Glen walked out on his own accord at that show and hasn't seen an ER room since his last encounter.

Snoop Dogg would be proud of Glen if he were to read this story. Maybe Mr. Broadus will read this someday and have a good laugh. Maybe he will even give Glen another shot at seeing him in concert. Life can play out any way it wants to, at any given time. The rules of life are simple. There are no rules. Approach it with as much positive thinking as possible. Laughter helps as well.

Life is like a box of chocolates. One day the box is full of sweetness. Then the other day the box is empty and there is nothing but sadness and despair. Chew on that, Gump.

Foo Fighters
in Claymation

This will be one of the few stories that is not mine, in the sense that I was not physically present for this. Most of the characters you have already met are the participants here. They have told this story so many times and with such enthusiasm that I had to include it. It is just that good and it fits in perfectly with the overall theme of this book.

I can't remember why Ava and I were not in Southern California with all our friends for this story. We might have had a conflict in schedule or were stuck at work. Back then I was working every other weekend with my finance gig. Sucked, working crazy hour more than paid the bills. I was sad though. I remember wanting to go to this festival.

My friends George, Frank, and Murray were all getting together for a massive concert being held in Los Angeles. The annual KROQ Weenie Roast. Our other close friends and their wives, who all happened to be living in the LA and San Diego area, were also meeting up with them. One wife was bringing a friend from Montana, and the other wife was bringing some work friends. It was the married folks bringing in the single ladies for the single dudes. Perfect conditions for an awesome story to unfold.

While I was sad that Ava and I could not make it on this trip, I was happy for the rest of the crew to get a much needed get together. I knew just by the sheer amount of raw brain power involved in this trip there would be no way it could fail to entertain. It achieved that expectation and then some.

Morning (Part 1):

As was always customary with our group of friends, we would always try to get together a day or two before the main event that brought us together. This always allowed for catching up and not feeling rushed. This motley crew and their two lovely wives got together the Friday night prior to the big extravaganza that was happening on Saturday and Sunday.

As usual they all got together and busted out all the new and old stories. Like clockwork the wives retired early to get some sleep and let the boys become less functional forms of society. Nothing too insane came about that night. They had way too much to drink, told terrible stories, and poked fun at each other about their insecurities. This groups typical modus operandum when then get together. The next day things would change.

With a solid four or five hours of inebriated sleep, they all started their morning wake up rituals. The wives were up scolding their husbands for waking them up in the middle of the night and telling them to get their asses up, so they didn't miss the show. Still drunk from the night before the guys woke each other up and quickly began clearing their aching heads with some mimosas and orange beers. Keep the party going as they would always say.

The Weenie Roast was notorious for bringing in huge rock and alt rock bands for a full day of concert utopia. This particular year was a doozy. Some of the biggest and most popular bands from the past few years were playing. The concerts from the prior years had been epic with artists such as The Foo Fighters, Stone Temple Pilots, Black Sabbath, Korn, Red Hot Chili Peppers, Blink 182, and Metallica. It was a who's who of bands at the top of their respective rock and alternative genres. It was a must see and it was always sold out. It only got bigger and bigger every year.

It was also inevitably a shit show. We are talking about 30,000 plus fans filled into a compact venue. These fans were almost either drunk off their skunk or high as a kite. It was that type of give and take environment. It was just too long of a festival day to not over imbibe past your minimum standards.

Lucky for most of the group, Glen's wife Caliente, was employed with a pretty large independent music label. The reason they were all on this expedition was because of Caliente. She had scored the group all backstage passes as well as center aisle seats. You can see why I was so sad to missing out on this.

Most of this group has zero reason to really be at this type of music festival. Half of them had no idea how to even pronounce some of the bands playing. Glen was a huge fan of older music in his parent's era, like the Glenn Miller Orchestra. Caliente? Well, she was really into old school country, blues, and jazz. Her idea of a mosh pit was at a Dave Matthews Band concert. Frank and Murray fit in though. Those guys were about as metal as metal gets. They were the two guys that still rode Greyhound busses around the Pacific Northwest while banging out to Megadeth. These two were ready for a night of screaming treble in their ears and maybe a side of Satan if he was surfing the crowd. George was into modern country and any song that they played on the radio 100 times. He was a big fan of repeating popular songs until you wanted to break the CD he was listening to. Barney was just there to support his wife. He was more into gangsta rap.

They would always tell anyone that would listen that the best part of that night wasn't the fact they got to go backstage and see up and coming artists like Pink. It wasn't the fact that George got to do a one on one ping-pong match with Travis Barker of Blink 182 fame. Nope. The best part was that they were all together for the first time in many, many years and it was just like stepping back into college. Something I often related to but not on this trip.

The outside of the arena was mix up of extreme sports types with a hint of a drunk uncle who got free tickets because his company couldn't give them away. Nothing made sense here. It was homies from the Green Goblin crew riding their dirt bikes doing nothing but wheelies around cotton candy cart vendors. It was Coachella before Coachella got acid dubstep rock. The Weenie Roast was the start of weekend festivals. the one thing that shocked almost everyone in the group that weekend was the number of drugs that were openly used.

While a few of my friends were holier than thou type against that drug culture, I would like to make a blanket statement. I don't give two fucks who does what to their own bodies in their own lifetime. You want to snort up all of Bolivia and Peru in one night? Too late, my buddy Christian Ellis has already been there and done that. I am totally fine with the options people choose for themselves. If it doesn't directly affect me then giddy up. Do what you got to do. There are some limitations, however. Everyone should know their own limitations before doing anything. You should also know your friends well enough that if you need to dissuade such them from going overboard then that's your duty. But sometimes that just can't or won't happen.

As the group walked into the stadium, they all should have taken the above advice.

Afternoon (start of concert):

The crew had broken off in typical 7th grade dance form. The girls went one way and the boys bought beer and went the other way. They would meet back at their seats in an hour or so. This was the right option for this mix of random people. You had the metalheads and DARE graduates, Frank and Murray. Then you had the "will do anything for a drink" attitude of George and Barney. Then you had Glen and his "Christian CEO" mentality.

The women were fine leaving the boys. The night prior the wives tried to introduce their friend from Montana, Anna Pease, to single guy George. It was disastrous to say the least. Something happened and then something happened on top of that and then somehow there was George, spilling an entire bottle of red Cab on his arranged date from Montana. In 10 out of 10 cultures that behavior was just taboo. The second day the wives were determined to get Anna to forget the prior events and give George another shot. The wives wanted nothing more than for George to find a good woman and settle in like a hibernating bear.

The kink in the wives' plan was that Chris had made it to town. He was fresh off his recent divorce and was prowling for that next commitment. Anna told the wives that she thought Chris looked like her best friend, who happened to bat for the other team. Anna always wanted that friend, but it was never going to happen unless Anna got an operation. The wives assured Anna that Chris liked his woman. He would fall in love with a girl if she simply offered him a Coke. The wives' sneaky plan to get Anna to fall in love with George was going nowhere.

There was Frank, Chris, George and Murray that were all aboard the single for life train. They were prowling the stadium harder than Brett Kavanaugh after a few football practice brewskies. They were on a mission to make some young ladies fall head over heels for their Montana charm and Mississippi good looks. Glen and Barney hung with them as much as possible, but they knew their time with the single crew was going to get cut short. They need to get back to the wives and their buddies.

One of the first bands the entire group could relate to came on. Sugar Ray was taking center stage. Glen, George and Barney scurried back to their seats so they could watch the ladies shake it to Sugar Ray's number one hit "Every Morning". The crew, minus the three single dudes, found their respective seats. They were awesome seats. Caliente had scored big time with her temporary company. They were four rows in front of the stage. There, in all his coiffed highlights glory, Mark Mc-Grath was shaking his hips right at their heads. The girls of course were mesmerized. Two of them had been through the Miss USA pageants back home in Montana. They had not seen this type of stardom since their days in the pageant. The boys were another story.

Barney was in his own little cocoon. He usually became that way after three white Zinfandels. He was shaking his head to some unknown Sugar Ray song and grinding his pelvis on the metal chair in front of him. Glen was looking every which way but loose. He had gobbled down his seventh whiskey and coke and the only thing on his face was a blank stare. He was well on his way to blackout city.

George was in his own personal party. He had noticed some interesting smells coming from the five younger kids sitting directly ahead of their group. He knew that smell. It took him all the way back to his infamous college years. It was the Devil's weed. The funky Skunk. The Mary Jane. George was buzzing hard from his fifteen plus beers and five shots of Fireball. It was time to "up the bet" as he famously put it. He was going to meet some new friends.

George sauntered over to the expanding cloud cover next to their seats. The younger gentlemen that were partaking in their extracurricular activities looked at George and realized he was not the police. Just like most strangers do at huge concerts, they offered to share their treasure trove with him. The rest of the party was in full on drunk dance mode and could not be bothered with George's disappearance. Anna Pease saw what George was up to though. She just looked at him with disgust and moved on to a new man in the crowd. What she didn't know was this was simply George's way of compensating for his extreme shyness around pretty women. It had been a few years since he last had any meaningful relations. Rosy Palm did not count. The dry spell for George was real. That's not an excuse, just an explanation.

When George invited himself into this roundabout of dudes, he figured he might as well make the best of it. He decided he did not want to be just one of the eight guys that were passing the puff around the circle. Nope. George was going to "up the bet" in his own way. He changed into an imaginary ninja so that these newfound youngsters would not see what he was up to. What he was doing was inserting himself into every other puff position. When one of these strangers would smoke up, then pass it to their friend, and then pass it to George. Then the same rotation would happen. One stranger, then their friend and then George somehow show up in the third spot. George would run around the circle like a kindergarten kid and make himself available every third pass rotation. Bless that George; he always ran into situations without any real plan or regard. I think that is where he and I connected the most: reckless abandon.

Little did George know that this Bob Marley joint that he was aggressively partaking in was laced with something extra. To this day no one knows what exactly that extra fun was, but given the outcome of the night, it's safe to say that it was Angel Dust, PCP, or Mescaline. Something with a lot of extra kick to get someone's night to another level. George of course finished off the Rastafarian plant in copious fashion. The young little hoodlums looked up to George at that moment. They had never seen someone take so much laced drugs. That's at least the way George tells that part of the story to everyone that will listen. I am guessing those kids were wondering why old Pauly Shore just wheezed their juice.

Now came the real fun part. George's own little trip.

By the time his escapade was over the concert was about halfway done. The group had splintered and were basically doing their own thing. The girls had lost interest in the men and were in their own party. Then there was George all by his lonesome.

To hear George, tell the story, it was very simple. He only remembers bits and parts of the next six or so hours. He knows he got lost from the group, even though they were a few feet away from his drum circle. He remembers talking to multiple new friends, but those new friends were not very helpful. Their words were literally coming from their mouths. He was seeing the visual patterns of what they were saying but it was not registering. The one thing he remembered vividly was that after some time the band Korn came on. He also remembered that he had somehow moved from the ground level seats to the top rows of the stadium. Not anywhere close to where he was supposed to be.

He was with some new friends now, telling them all about his life and why they should listen to his worldly, twenty-seven-year-old advice. He was on cloud nine, or some sort of cloud. Or in the clouds. These are all possibilities as he was the only one around to verify the facts. The one thing he absolutely knows was true and still can recount to this very day is that when he finally focused on the band, he noticed something was off. The entire performance was something he was not used to. Everything he was watching was in Claymation. You know, like that old Rudolph the Red Nosed Reindeer show from the 50's that plays every Christmas? Or like the old MTV celebrity deathmatch fights? Yeah, his entire Korn concert experience was in Claymation. This was slowly becoming the best night of his life.

Eventually he started coming down from his super high and he saw that the final band was playing. He was now out in the commons area behind the main stage. He started to get some semblance of his bearings and made a strategic move back to his seat. When he showed up, the group had all reassembled and had the "where have you been" look on their faces. Except for Anna. She was so over his shit. He was of course well on his way to confidence-vile and played it off like he had only been gone about a half hour.

Now when I discussed this same story with Barney and Glen and their wives, they all were not on the same wavelength and in sync with the same story of George tells everyone. Their story was way funnier and radically different than Georges watered down version.

Barney told me the minute that Anna Pease lost interest in our boy George, that he was embarrassed and wanted to move on from her proximity. He drowned himself in multiple Fireball shots and immediately left the group. He told the couples that he was going to look for Frank, Murray and Chris to see what they were up to. What George did not know was that he only moved a mere ten feet from Barney and Glen. He did not move on to find the single boys. He really did think he was a ninja, and no one could see him. The next part was the only part that matched up between the two tales. Barney said he watched George go up to this group of teenagers and bully his way into the smoke circle. To Barneys amazement, they watched George become accepted into his new social circle. He then watched George do some sort or rain dance around the circle of guys. Glen was the one that pointed out that George was not dancing. He was stealing hits off this group of high school kids.

What happened after that was also drastically different than what George had told everyone. They watched him look around the crowded concert floor and they knew that he was in no mood to come back to his pre-arranged date. They also all agreed that was good for both George and Anna. Anna's church values did not mesh well with George's walk with the Devil attitude.

Barney said he watched George walk to the front of the stage, which at this point had Blink 182 playing their set. Barney then watched George curiously walk over to a large trash can near the side stage, crouch down, and hide behind it. Barney punched Glen in the nuts as the music was too loud to talk. Glen was stunned but looked to where Barney was pointing to. Glen got to watch the oddity of George's actions unfold.

They were all good enough friends to make sure that he was ok, but they wanted to see where this carnival ride was headed. For about half an hour, George did not come out of crouching tiger mode near this trash can. When he was later asked what he was doing, he would tell everyone that the multiple weed shots hit him way harder than he expected. This was the point where he could only see everything in Claymation. Georges tripped out senses were too heightened. He had no idea what was going on. Eventually George came back to reality and found his way back to the group.

As the group was leaving the concert, they ran into the rest of the party. Frank and Murray were smitten with a group of females they had befriended and watched the concert with. That short exchange had given just the right amount of time for George to relapse and find himself in his next mischief moment. Glen and Barney looked around quick and found George within minutes. He was tip toeing over to a side trailer. One of the band's trailers.

Barney and Glen told the group to hold tight. They knew they were too late to stop George. They could only hope to contain him.

When they ran up to the trailer, they saw the band's name scrawled on the front door. The fucking Foo Fighters. They also saw that George was already in the trailer and had helped himself to a six pack of beer in the fridge. George walked out and threw a beer to each of the guys.

Someday George is going to have to pay them back twenty-fold. Glen and Barney were able to wrangle him out of the trailer before security saw anything or even worse, before the band showed up. The only positive was they at least got beers for the road.

A Tale of Two Weenies

Later that night (Part 2):

The boys had dropped off the ladies as they wanted nothing more to do with the dumb decisions that were taking place. Which was fine with the guys. They knew that there was plenty of time to keep the good times rolling.

The problem was that Murray and Frank were madly in love by the end of the Weenie Roast festival. Chris was already moving in with the girl he just met. Par for the course with Chris. The mix of perfume and concert sweat soaked clothes was too enticing. They convinced the married guys and George to tag along to a house party they had been invited to. Technically only Frank and Murray had been invited, not the other four dudes. Of course, that part was never communicated.

When they all arrived at the party, they found themselves back in familiar territory. This was a raging classic college party with a house that was packed to capacity people half their age. The ladies that had invited them were there, but only half of the original pack. Frank and Murray's choices were slimming. Thankfully Chris had already proposed to his newest girlfriend. That boy moves fast. Good news for the single guys. That was one less person to compete with.

They immediately surround their dates from the concert and start the early stages of hooking up. At some point early in the party, Frank was unfortunately rejected by one of these girls. He swore he was going to hook up. He then took it upon himself to wallow in a few shots with George. The alcohol led him to become very relaxed his current unfamiliar surroundings. He went to find a bathroom and stumbled upon a laundry room. When George next saw Frank he nearly spit his beer out of his nose. Frank rolled out of the back-laundry room with a dirty pair of girl's panties over his head. Frank had watched his formal buddy, Dick, do the same many years ago. Dick had got laughs form that party, so Frank assumed the same would happen with his take on the joke. He did not get any laughs. Some of the party goers quickly left the kitchen. Frank threw the panties quickly back in the dirty laundry. It could only go downhill from that point.

When Murray met up with the rest of the guys, they were all starting to get into a little bit of a who's smarter contest with the young party goers. Murray hated anyone younger than 50 so he decided to step away from those conversations. He took George aside and told him he needed his help with something. He needed George to find sharpie. Preferably black but any color would do. He had a mission for the two of them. George's peyote laced weed started to kick back in and he was feeling an artistic revival. He scampered off to find their tool of choice. It took him less than a minute to locate a sharpie.

Murray brought George back to an open hallway near the back of the home. There, passed out on the first set of stairs, was one of the girls from Weenie Roast. George knew exactly what Murray was intending.

They were going to marker up this poor girl. Hopefully your mind did not shift to something darker there. While my friends can be jerks from time to time, they all grew up with strong mothers. They were taught the lines they never cross. They all know the difference between funny and taking it to far. All our mothers put up with our stupidity, but only to a point. This was innocent fun they were about to embark in.

After they had sufficiently given this lovely girl a proper face painting, they snuck back to the rest of the friends. At that point, it was time to call it quits at the raging party. They found the guys in the kitchen trying to take shot for shot with the college aged kids. This was a disaster waiting to happen.

Just as Murray convinced the other guys that it was time to make an exit, they suddenly found themselves in a pickle. From out of nowhere the whole party heard an ear-piercing scream. At first, they thought someone was getting killed. Like in the movies the needle on the record scratched the music to an abrupt halt. Everyone was looking towards the hallway that George and Murray had recently emerged from.

"What the fuck!!! Who the fuck wrote the fuck all over me!!! I am about to kill someone."

The party girl had come to. She was found by one of her friends checking in on her. The second she saw herself in the mirror she understandably flipped her lid. She was glaring at my group of friends as they were the few outsiders not known in this packed house. Also, my friends' stealth mode detectors are all broken. Severely broken. One of her friends saw them come from the hallway. Duh.

She knew immediately it had to be them. She went over to George first. As she yelled at him while her friend held her back, his prior mescaline laced sinsemilla decided once again. His waves were picking terrible times to roll his brain. He was embarrassed and confused. He reacted with what came first into his head. He immediately pointed to Murray and simply said "He did it".

How they all didn't get into a brawl is beyond me. Most of my friends have some size to them. They also all have experience in fist fights from growing up. Murray was not the right one to get blamed. The last fight he got in he broke his thumb because he tucked it into his throwing punch. They were also grossly outnumbered. There were about 20 guys to each one of my buddies. Plus, they found out Chris had eloped already. He left hours ago on his way to Vegas *(allegedly).

As the guys in the party started yelling at my friends and calling them unfathomable names, they decided it was the best to get the fuck outta Dodge.

Murray stood outside on the corner of the street right in front of the house. He watched as his asshole friends getting ejected from the party. Even though racist insults were being thrown his way as well as bottles, bananas, and maybe even a dildo, he had to laugh at the absurdity of it all. Or maybe he was laughing at the very large vagina that he and George had drawn on this poor girl. He collected the party and got them all into a nearby cab just as a group of young guys came running up. They hightailed it out just in time to avoid any real major confrontations. As they all laughed about the entire set of circumstances that entire day Barney yelled at the cab driver to stop.

There was Chris. He was walking all by himself down the road miles away from the party. He jumped in and told the group that they would not be getting an invite to his after-wedding party. It only took a few miles for his girlfriend to sober up and decide that she was too young to get married.

Some days are worth every risk taken to get yourself or someone else to laugh. Unless you are doing random drug circles with unknown drugs or fucking with strangers that you have never met. Proceed with caution in either of those situations.

!

While doing research (aka: conversations with all parties involved) for this book I had a ton of feedback. I also had so many people tell me "this" or "that" and their story that should be included in this book. My response was always the same.

While their request was genuine and indeed there was humor in the story they told, I always held reservation. Sometimes the story they wanted me to tell wasn't mine to tell. I was always adamant that they should start writing themselves and put out their own book. With those stories. Other times those stories were funny for one moment but what led up to that funny moment was dull as fuck. Not relatable to the audience. Lastly, some stories just do not need to be told. Those are the vault stories.

I never want to bring harm to any person within these pages or within my life. Living life to the fullest is a fantastic gift that each of us have been given. You can absolutely poke fun at those you care about. You can even describe situations with more flare than what was present. If the core truth of the story remains, and it doesn't hurt anyone involved. Then, I believe the presentation is fair game.

All this shit I spewed above is because I am trying to tell you something. I may have taken some liberties with these truths. The audience needs a ride to get to the destination. Nothing is perfect and that is the core of what this book is about. Little imperfections that make every single one of us special. I love all of you and as you sit there and remember your own true, funny, crazy stories from your own past I want you to know one thing.

Chris really didn't elope that night. He swung and he struck out. He really has been married four times as of this writing though. That shit's the truth.

PAPA SMURF'S JOB INTERVIEW

Fraternity life was an interesting experience. I know the general public's view of fraternity men is in the basement these days. I can't argue with that that. With multiple alcohol related deaths, chapters being shut down monthly, and of course high-profile politicians behaving poorly, fraternities' negative reputations are justified.

I have a slightly different perspective because of my personal experience in a fraternity. Not every fraternity is the same and not every group of men living that lifestyle are the same. For me, the comradery of group of young men with vastly different backgrounds was fantastic. A few of my fraternity brothers were friends from high school, but the majority were new people from all parts of the country. These men remain part of my life today.

This was a fraternity in Montana. A small school by any means. The student population hovered right around 12,000. We only had six fraternities the time, not the 20 or more that you see at larger schools. It looked a little different than the typical fraternity stereotype. We had every walk of life living there, which is what made it so wonderful.

Sadly, even though our fraternity had been on campus since 1908, the actual house we lived in had seen better days. Additionally, the early nineties were a period of decline for Greek organizations. People viewed fraternities and sororities as outdated institutions that perpetuated elitism and uniformity. The cultural movement at the time was individualism and rebelling against norms and systemic practices. The fraternity was part of that system. Our humble animal house didn't feel like it though. We were a collective of east coast hippie stoners, west coast extroverts, Midwest jocks, artists, musicians, activists, and eggheads. A truly eclectic group of young idiots.

When I say we were idiots, I say that with the utmost sincerity of being tongue in cheek. We had some very, very bright young guys that have since founded companies and gone to work for very large corporations. No, when I say we were idiots I should point out that most 18 to 24-year-old men tend to be idiots because according to Jean Piaget our formal operational skills are not yet fully developed. We think we are all invincible and that we can't possibly be wrong. We find out later how wrong we really were and learn to live with the regret of those poor decisions.

One of the most idiotic things that my close friends from high school and I started doing way back in the day and, I admit, still do today is to draw on each other's faces. If you fall asleep too early you run the risk of being "Sharpied. I don't remember who started this amazing game, but at age 43 we still find it hilarious. I know it's dumb and it can be categorized as infantile humor.

Well, it's only dumb if you are on the receiving end of it. If you are on the giving side, then it's fantastic!

The game of "Sharpied" is simple: if you are with a group of friends, and you are out enjoying your time together, then you are expected to stay up as long as possible to keep the party going. It could be anywhere. A simple house party, a late-night game of Poker, a club or bar, or even at a very early morning breakfast. Generally, the game revolves around drinking but not necessarily. Many players have been in various states of mind. There are very few rules to the game. If you happen to over imbibe, or simply can no longer hang with the crew, and you pass out in a common area then you become fair game to the other participants. Those participants then locate some black or colored markers and go to town with basic artwork on the poor soul who decides to pass out near them. The one hard and fast rule is that you generally cannot Sharpie someone who makes it to their own bed and locks the door behind them. You also can not physically hold someone down or against their will. If they wake up and realize what is going on, you must stop.

I don't think I need to tell all of you that rules are meant to be broken. In most cases. Or at least stretched. This is how we create things that others say are impossible. In this story, the rules were stretched. It was a third-party participant that allowed the stretch of these rules. She was an absolute gem for all the help.

One dark and not stormy night in the middle of an above normal temperature spell, the entire fraternity decided to go out and enjoy each other's company in the local bars. Finals were almost over and a lot of us were finished and had nothing else to do but work and celebrate the end of another great year. It was very rare that most of us all ended up at the same place on late nights. We all had different tastes and were usually drawn to various late-night establishments. Yet that night, we all ended up together and having an absolute blast. It was one of those perfect nights with no drama and plenty of positive vibes.

One of my stalwart supporters, George, was in his typical inebriated state. Nothing crazy, but he was on top of his drinking game. He was making friends at every turn and buying shots and drinks for the entire house. Well, his mother's credit card was buying those drinks. So, thanks to Sue for many of those free drink nights. I've got to give credit where credit is due.

George was happy, and it wasn't just because of the amount of alcohol he was consuming. He was riding on some very positive things going on in his life. He had technically passed all his courses that year. Considering he only made it to about 20% of his weekly lectures, it was something of a miracle. He did have a knack for cramming at the last minute for tests. He also had a girlfriend. He was in a relationship with a gal pal he had known for a couple years and they were compatible on many levels. They shared a love for many things: inebriation, food, and the same kinks in and out of the bedroom. To complete the trifecta, George had an interview scheduled for a bouncer position at his favorite downtown bar, Bodega. George was on fire and hitting on all cylinders.

Oddly, George was nowhere to be seen, as the bar announced its last call for alcohol. Half of the guys from our house had taken off, but there was still a large handful of us trying our luck at finding a late-night date. This, as usual, ended with most of us going home to late night snacks and more bullshit. The women generally disappeared as they wanted nothing to do with a bunch of drunken idiots. Totally understandable.

As we walked back to the house that night, we were talking about keeping the party going. We stopped at the local convenience store on the way back and picked up a few cases. We had the idea that if we bought more alcohol back to the house, we could stop by and ask some of our sorority sisters if they wanted to come back and keep the party flowing. Which of course never happened.

When we staggered onto the front lawn of our fraternity house, we realized a couple things. Some of the guys that had left early were already on the front porch with some of their lady friends. They had the same idea we did, they had just left a little early and started the party at the house instead of closing the Bodega. We also noticed that they were talking to a couple of adults. We thought maybe we were getting into trouble with the neighbors again as they did not appreciate some of our late-night parties. It happened to be our celebrity neighbor who had moved in a few months prior, Andie MacDowell. She and her husband were coming back from a Gala function and saw a few of the guys and ladies hanging out and thought it would be nice to share a neighborly drink. She was cool like that and was one of our favorite neighbors.

The second thing we noticed was that George was not in his usual spot on the front stoop. I asked one of our roommates if they had seen George. We wanted to make sure he was safe and sound. We are at least good for that as fraternity brothers. Never leave a man behind.

Sure enough, they said that he had stumbled in about a half an hour ago with his girlfriend, garbled some sort of joke, and then proceeded to tell everyone around him that he and his lady friend were going to head up to his room and bang the brains out of each other. He also made sure to tell them that if any of us assholes come home and tried to get him up that he would have his door triple locked and it would be futile. That comment only made it worse for George.

We were not a quiet bunch, especially as we stumbled up the stairs to wake our little buddy up. He was due to keep the party going. On the three flights we were parading up, we managed to grab a few other brothers to come help wake up George. I get a little jealous writing these words. Who doesn't want a parade of ten of your good friends walking into your love chamber to wake you up? – said every intimately involved girlfriend/boyfriend ever.

When we arrived at his darkened closed door, we were surprised that it was not dead bolted. Just like vampires being invited into their prey's home, the ten of us not so quietly entered his den of joy. Luckily, his girlfriend was somewhat awake and was not furious. She was decent and expecting the assholes. We all exchanged pleasantries and then asked if it was at all possible for our good buddy could come out and play. Being fair-weathered to the lot of us, she said she would gladly accept the invitation for both. However, the rather intense "talk" the two of them had before we barged in had done him in. He was dead to the world. His well-timed, earth shattering snores were enough to convince us that he was out of commission.

We then thought of something that would break the awkward silence of his buddies in his room in a very private moment. We asked if she minded if we possibly did a little artwork on our friend. Kind of like texting. Simply to let him know we were in the area looking for him. He wasn't home, so we left a message. This was way before the time of mass cell phones and easy connectivity. This was the old way to "text a buddy."

The problem was that we had way too many leaders in the room. Too many people wanted to tag their piece of property, including his girlfriend. Which is when we all knew that it was ok. If his girlfriend was ok with the stupidity, then we knew George would get a kick out of it the next day.

When we all backed away, we saw nothing short of a masterpiece. A collective Salvador Dali if you will. George would strongly disagree with us all. Someone had the foresight to tell the room he was grabbing his disposable camera and we all needed to pose for a group pic with George. I have tried, unsuccessfully, for the past year to acquire that photo. I have seen it, and I can say it was clearly a masterpiece. The smiles on those twelve peoples' faces (not my face of course) were priceless. There is a price. If any of my buddies out there reading this are in possession of said photo, please send me that shit. I will compensate you in some fashion.

As we all slunk out of George's room, we gave his girlfriend a high five and the Blue Steel look that both said, "We appreciate your cooperation in this project," mixed with "now, don't say shit." And we all went to bed and rested our weary heads.

That next morning was a real mother fucker. Not because of the mind piercing growl coming from outside our doors. Not because of the loud smashing on each and everyone's doors. But because of what Karma was about to do to me.

George was up. George had gone potty. George remembered at precisely 7 AM, when he awoke from his drunken, sex induced slumber, that he had an interview for his dream job in two hours. George also realized he was blue from head to toe. I mean, Sharpie blue in places that should not have been Sharpied period. Somehow the gang made the great decision to not mark up his face that much as the artwork might stay hidden longer. The mistake we made was that we forgot he was next to naked when we dabbled in body painting for the first time. We also grossly mistook his ability to get up and put on some clothes before he wandered out to his morning bathroom break.

So, there I was. Fearfully trapped in the communal shower down in the basement, right next to Zahn's dungeon, listening to the loudest yelling and banging around that this poor house of almost 100 years had probably ever seen. There was an angry Kodiak bear coming down the hall, and it was heading straight to the shower. Directly in my very vulnerable direction.

As I heard George yelling at random people, and mostly to no one at all, I caught something that I had forgotten. I think it was about the thirtieth time I heard him say, "Really cool, you fucking assholes! I have a job interview in a fucking hour. If I don't get the job, it's because of you fuckheads!" Then I remembered that indeed he told me about his dream employer finally granting him an interview for a starter position. I felt bad for about the two hundred thirty-two seconds that I heard his rant on the way to the shower.

This was one of like four times I thought George might have finally blown his last fuse and was ready to go over the edge on someone. I happened to be the only someone to be in that class six hurricane's way. I was trapped with no way of getting out of the communal shower. The only exit was the same entrance my good friend was about to appear from. It was time to go into survival mode. My own survival. I knew what I had to do. I had to lie my fucking ass off.

When George emerged through the steam of my shower, his eyes were a shade of Evil Devil red. I limply asked him how his night was and why he didn't meet up with me to head home. He called my bluff, as this was a man, I had known for the past 13 years. After what I can only describe as a mixture of his internal self-control trying to fend off his Exorcist demon and many, many derogatory words hurled in my direction, he was calm enough to put together a normal conversation. Well, as normal as two dudes, stark naked in a communal shower, screaming at each other can be.

He wanted to know who the culprits were. He knew I was involved even though my denials were consistent. I simply lied and told him the people I saw awake when I came home. Besides, I reminded him, I knew the rules of the game. No disrespect in your own place of slumber, unless someone else who shares that space offers an invitation. The blood pact. That's when he described his dislike for his current girlfriend and how she betrayed him as she let a bunch of idiots into his abode.

It was one of the most uncomfortable situations I have ever been in. Naked. Vulnerable. Lying my ass off to save a well-deserved beating. It was nearly impossible to look at this naked, hairy man who resembled a certain famous Seinfeld character, and not bust out laughing. The words written across his body, actually very long sentences written across his body. An absolute wonderment of beautiful blue. I had to feign coughing so that my burst of laughter was quelled.

He didn't really buy my story of denial. But he also couldn't prove anything. Instead he went on to the "make me feel guilty" phase. He described in detail that he had an interview in less than 30 minutes and his whole fucking body looked like something out of the Smurf village. The only saving grace was that his face was not marked up too much and he was able to get off the little that was on there.

Then Karma kicked in. Big time.

Since I was the only one in the shower, he needed some real help. His guilt game was strong. Let it be known that if it had not been for my own guilty conscience or the fact that my good friend was worried about potentially losing his future job of a lifetime, I would have "noped" the fuck out of that shower. But alas, I was stuck. I had to oblige.

There I was, using his shower loofah to fiercely scrub his back. He was directing me to get all the blue off. It is something I never want to do again. It was my penance. I felt horrible; that blue Sharpie was not coming off. In fact, it was just smearing all over his body to give the full effect of an early member of the Blue Man group.

When I told him nothing was working and the blue was getting worse, the beast from the underworld again emerged. As he was yelling and screaming incoherently, I told him to calm down. There was always a solution. Even if that solution is not the most comfortable or viable. I told him that even though it was July and the temperature was going to be scorching that day, there was a way to hide the distinct blue emanating from his skin. He still had his winter clothes packed away upstairs. There were options.

Generally, the only people who can pull off a solid black turtleneck, regardless of month of the year, are Dwayne "The Rock" Johnson and intravenous drug users. But this was before The Rock was a household name, so Heroin chic it was. There was no other choice.

When I saw George walk down to the foyer, I couldn't help but burst out in full laughter. It was just too much. He was wearing long, dark jeans and a full turtleneck. On his hands were ski gloves. What the actual fuck was I witnessing? It was like the rebirth of Dexter Rutecki.

He told me to fuck off and pushed me onto the couch in the front room and stomped out the door.

He got the fucking job.

His dream of bouncing at the front door of the local college bar, Bodega, was realized. When I asked how the hell he pulled the whole thing off and got the owner to give him a chance. He simply told me that when he sat down to talk with Bob, the owner, he decided to lay it all out and tell him why he looked like an extra from "Hot Dog" the movie. There ended up being no need.

Bob simply took one look and told George that his son had vouched for him and that was good enough. He was getting the job. It didn't hurt that George had spent a small fortune in that very bar throughout his college career. The least Bob could do was let him earn some of it back. Bob told him one last thing. He didn't know why George was dressed like he was headed to an MTV show being filmed in the Arctic circle when it was close to 90 degrees at noon, but if there was a story to it, Bob did not want to know anything. He felt that if the job meant that much for George to dress up like he was going to a ski party, then that commitment was good enough to bounce some assholes out of his bar.

And that my friend, is how Papa Smurf acquired his dream job. He has since moved on to become successful in love and life. Probably only because he was dressed for success on that very important day.

JINGLE BALLS, JINGLE BELLS, JINGLE ALL THE WAY

The bond of friendship is an interesting one. It can be a delicate dance along the path of life. The hope is that the bond is strong enough to withstand the glass that is sometimes littered on the path because there will be times when there is absolutely no way to not step on that glass and you veer off the path.

My friendship with Chris is one fraught with all the great things of a great friend. To be fair, I have had many amazing and long friendships in my life. I am beyond lucky in the friend department. My family is included in those close bonds. My friends became my family and so all my people are intertwined. I am dedicating this book to not only family, but also to random strangers that took a chance on Chance. Cheers to every one of you. You know who you are. Back to Chris. Good old' Chris McDonaldson.

Chris was my closest friend while we were growing up in our formative and very corruptible years. Yes, George, Frank, and Murray were there from the very beginning as well, but Chris and I had a different vibe together. Our connection was mainly wrapped up in our love of late eighties and early nineties gangsta rap and our lack of discretionary funds. We got along with everyone. We hated being part of a clique, even though we were in that clique balls deeps.

Chris was a great guy. Honestly, too great of a guy, especially when it came to the ladies in his life. He often told them things they didn't even want to know. This is Ross from "Friends." It was wonderful that he was now a couple years removed from his first marriage and was back in Missoula for the Christmas holidays.

Ava and I, most of my family, and some other close friends were also home for Christmas. Hell, even my little sister, Arianna, was back in town. She had my two little nieces with her, and it was just one of those family holiday get togethers where everything was perfect. Even the tree my dad put up that year was magical.

This was Ava's fifth or so Christmas with everyone and they seemed to all be getting astronomically better each year. How could they get worse?

My father, Red, was your wonderfully stereotypical, born in the forties, type of gentlemen. He had the still silence of a man with too many thoughts, yet the inebriated swagger of a master auctioneer at the end of his gala shift. What I am trying to say is my dad, in all his stubbornness and unwillingness to change his ways, is still my dad. He taught me a lot more than he realizes. In fact, I must publicly, and possibly legally, set the record straight about something I said in extreme error in my previous book.

I may or may not have told the world (as of this printing only six of the seven continents) that it was my mother who gave me the love for the Devil's syrup, aka booze. The day before I was to publish my very first book, I had sent my mother a copy of the final draft. I told her it was coming out whether the family liked it or not. Or whether my wife liked it or not. Or whether my in-laws liked it or not. You get the point. That fact was a little misguided and misconstrued. While my mother enjoys a nice glass of wine, she is very good at holding her own and drinking with restraint. So, I can now publicly say my mother is not the reason her youngest child has a bit too much familiarity with booze.

My close relationship with alcohol comes directly from my father. He can put away more scotch than a gaggle of Scots at a cask opening. He is the grandmaster of drinking and bullshitting. Growing up I can't think of a time that I saw him without a Scotch on the rocks or some sort of glass with alcohol in it. Dad, if you are reading this (which you are not supposed to be), Mom made me write this.

I also have another mea culpa. Contrary to popular opinion, it was not George's fault for me beginning to drink in high school. He was only 50% of the reason. I should also let my mom and dad know that the hidden beer they kept finding in the garage did not always belong to George. Sometimes it belonged to another friend that frequented our home. It's probably time to rat him out since he's the focus of this story.

Chris was the other half of the reason I started drinking so young. He was a magnet that I couldn't help but hang out and try new things with. George, Frank, and Murray began drinking before Chris and I did. They bullied us for a year to at least try a beer. So, when Chris folded like a weathered lawn chair in a category four hurricane, I reluctantly followed the group. Chris started boozing like the unforgotten McKenzie brother, I tried to keep up. When it came to Christmas, our core group could have a couple of beers as long as we stayed at home with our families. That tradition is still alive and well.

My family was all together for Christmas Eve. Ava was having a blast, and my mom and dad were in their glory entertaining all night. As usual, the kitchen was the epicenter for our family gathering. So, from lunch to late that night, most of us congregated there laughing, telling stories, and celebrating. The kids were doing their own thing elsewhere. They played video games and enjoyed quality cousin time. It was a great time for all.

By late Christmas Eve, things were winding down. My mom and dad had finished their standard three fights about something trivial. My friends had come and gone and so had our traditional gift exchange. Our friend gift exchange involved us finding the dumbest, crappiest gifts for each other and then exchanging them in front of our family. It's possible many of our nieces and nephews got their first look at grade F pornography and tasteless humor on t-shirts from those presentations. Luckily 90% of them grew up just fine. My apologies to the ones we might have slightly corrupted.

Chris had consumed copious amounts of holiday spirits and had decided he would take one of my parent's guest rooms and just get up early to go see his mom and dad on Christmas Day. He lucked out. Because Ava and I were childless at this time in our life, we only needed one room at my parents. My sister and her girls slept in the main room so there was plenty of room for Chris to crash.

As my father was being ushered up to bed by my mom, Ava, Chris, Arianna, and I stayed up a little later and played cards. We kept the small party going. Christmas Eve is a glorious time to forget your troubles and truly be merry. Sometime after midnight, Ava and I decided to call it a night. We were done and we knew with my sister's little ones in the house we would be up at the crack of dawn opening gifts. Chris headed upstairs, too. He wanted to get some sleep, have breakfast with my family, and then head out to see his own family.

The next morning, we woke up a little later than our typical Christmas Day tradition. When we finally made it downstairs, everyone was seated at the formal breakfast table. My dad was lurking in the kitchen making pancakes. As we sat around the table on that lovely Christmas morning, we noticed that someone was very obviously missing. Chris was nowhere to be seen.

I yelled up from the table for Chris to wake his ass up and come down for breakfast. There was no answer, he was being incredibly impolite. Even Ava, who is usually very relaxed and forgiving, thought it was weird that my best friend was not responding to my commands. He was a house guest and he was missing a delicious breakfast. About ten minutes later, my Mom asked me to go check on my buddy. I was irritated that I had to walk away from my pancakes.

As I got to the top of the stairs, I saw that his bedroom door was still shut. The hallway eerily darkened in the pale Montana winter dawn. I knocked on his door. He did answer, so at least this Christmas morning didn't end with death. He told me he had heard me earlier and he would be right down. I headed back to my pancakes. Chris was slowly trailing behind me. As he sat down, we all could sense a change in his usual demeanor. My verbal jabs didn't faze him, and he kept his eyes glued to the table. We didn't think much of it and enjoyed the rest of our breakfast. Chris immediately gathered his belongings and said a hurried goodbye to everyone. It was odd, but we dismissed his behavior as a simple hangover.

Seven years later I would learn, ironically at another Christmas gathering, a secret. My friends could not hold back anymore. Their willpower had given out. They proceeded to tell me all about my friend Chris and his special connection with my sister. I was horrified to learn of their tryst on my wedding night. My wife was laughing at my side, but she knew for a while. For me, it was the first of heard of their romantic interlude.

When the story surfaced, I knew I had to talk to my sister. Even she kept me in the dark; rightfully so, but usually she told me everything. I wanted to see what was true and what was just my friends trying to rile me up.

Arianna was very matter of fact about the whole thing. She thought I already knew and just chose to not talk about it. They were both consenting adults. Sure, there was about a seven-year age gap, but whatever. There was not much I could say or do. What was done, was done. While it gave me carte blanche to give them both shit about it for the rest of their lives, they were in the right. They had the hots for each other, and they knew that their best friend and their little brother, would never approve of it so they acted like adults and went on with it and kept everything quiet. Until my friends blabbed.

The real kicker of the story was the second part that my sister decided to divulge in that same conversation. Arianna reasoned that if I already knew about them hooking up at my wedding, I must know the story about my parent's house. I was about to get more than I bargained for, but I lied anyway. I told her I kind of remembered it, but she should refresh my memory.

Arianna said that a few years back, she had come home to my parents' house with her kids to celebrate Christmas. She had been living in Michigan with her current boyfriend and had not been back to Montana for quite a while. Apparently, she and her long-term boyfriend were on the outs and it looked like she may be moving back to Montana. I told her that of course I remembered all of that.

Then the real gold poured out. She mentioned that my friend, Chris, was back home as well. She explained why he had been so odd that Christmas morning. I was remembering it all clearly and was putting the puzzle together when she threw in the zinger.

She said the reason that Chris would not come down to breakfast was because he thought my father might kill him. Arianna described how when we all went to bed that night, she and Chris stayed up and started talking. One thing led to another and they rekindled some of those old loving feelings. But they really couldn't go anywhere private. His room was next to my parents' room. Arianna's kids were downstairs, so that was out. So, they got creative. They turned out the lights and went to the guest bathroom and laundry area off the kitchen. They at least shut the door.

Sure enough, as they became more entwined with their passion, they forgot that they weren't the only ones in the house. My dad drifted downstairs from his alcohol induced slumber, he swore he could hear some loud noises coming from the laundry room. He checked on the kids as he passed by and headed to the kitchen. It was dark, the girls were sound asleep. But he could still hear muffled, odd noises coming from the laundry room. He opened the door in pure wonder and, I am only guessing, the horror he saw scarred him forever.

Arianna said that when Dad opened the door, he had enough time to see them and then simply muttered something about not knowing anyone was up and shut the door. Both Chris and my sister were completely mortified. They heard my dad slowly stomp up the stairs before they slunk back out.

Arianna handled it like a champ. She never said a word and sat at that breakfast table almost daring my dad to say something. Chris, however, took the opposite approach - he simply went into hiding. But for whatever reason, my father did not come unglued. He made breakfast for everyone that next morning. He might have yelled a little louder for Chris to come down. But other than that, he never mentioned it to anyone, other than probably my mother. I think the very act of walking in and witnessing his youngest son's good friend thrusting into his daughter while sitting on the washing machine induced enough PTSD to last him a lifetime.

I did get my sister's and friend's permission to tell this Christmas tale. They both agreed. I, however, had to make a judgement call on my dad. He has a teasing nature about him, especially for his kids. For example, he told me my last book was good, but it wouldn't be a bestseller. I mean, he was right. But he didn't have to tease me about my passion project. He always likes to give me a good ribbing. So, I figured when he finally reads this chapter, he will know I paid him back. In fairness, I will also promise to not let my friends stay the night anymore.

Cheers, Dad!

Interfraternity Failure

My days in the fraternity were filled with wonderment on the grandest level. There was very rarely a dull day. There were so many characters and so many personalities added to a good amount of freedom and a mutual respect for one another.

I should take this time to dispel a couple of stereotypes that the public has about these types of organizations. I should also confirm that some of those stereotypes are correct. I blame both of those statements on John Belushi. For me, I took the value of meeting so many different people that I would not have otherwise met in complete reverence. I enjoyed the hell out of my time in my fraternity house. We were a fraternity in Montana. While we loosely, but legally, complied with our national headquarters, we were very much off the radar. Very few, except the men pledged and went to the U of M, even cared about either of the two Montana chapters. We were a blip in the 800 other chapters. These other chapters are housed a huge, nationally recognized universities. While we adhered to the general beliefs and code of ethics that nationals dictated, we were mostly left alone. We were mavericks. We were able to adopt our own identity.

It made complete sense when my good friends George, Murray, and Frank set their sights on joining the fraternity system right away as they started college. I decided to listen to the stereotypes and told them that I was not going to join a fraternity my freshman year. Plus, I was in a serious relationship from high school and even though my girlfriend was out of state doing her own thing in her own identity quest, we were still stupidly trying to make that long-distance thing work. I told those bozos that there was no chance she was going to let me join. I did ask, and that sentiment was absolutely relayed back to me from my then girlfriend. It was very convenient that come my sophomore year, I was in the midst of breaking up from my long term, out of state relationship.

At that time, I was still somewhat close with all my longtime friends, even though they were drifting off into new friendships made through the fraternity. Luckily, they always kept a door open for me and I met quite a few of their fraternity friends. It made me realize that I was wrong about what I thought fraternity people represented. Now don't get me wrong, there were some total asshats that fit the stereotypical, chauvinistic stereotype that we have all seen in Animal House. Overall, though, it was just a good group of guys that liked to have fun. Hell, even though I knew Glen in high school it really wasn't until I pledged the fraternity that I got to know him better and turned out he wasn't at all the person I had pegged him.

There was another person who guided me on my path to the fraternity. Big Zohan. He was the big brother that everyone wanted. He was 6'8" and built like a tank. I had only limited run ins in high school with him as he was a couple years older and ran in different circles. So, it was fitting that George brought him around quite a bit to help ease my mind about deciding to join the fraternity. One of the many mutual classes

George and I took at the U was Billiards. Every week George would come to class with Big Z. The three of us always had a blast. His strategy worked. I was sold on coming in for pledge week and testing the waters to see if fraternity life was for me.

I knew quite a few guys in the fraternity by the time I joined. There were over 30 guys living in the house and then another 15 or so living out of the house. When I made the decision to pledge with ten other gentlemen, it was a pretty easy social scene for me to adapt to. I mean, I was already working my butt off waiting tables which required a whole different level of socializing just to make some money. It was a great fit, and brother Zohan always took the new guys under his wing. He was one of the few people in the house that had the same taste in underground rappers that I did. It made it all the easier to hang out and click with the big fella. This homeboy grew up in the backwoods of our hometown. He knew a thing or two about getting down and dirty. This would come in handy many times throughout the years of our friendship.

One of the other reasons I hung out with big Z was that he had the same creative misdirection that I had during those formative early college years. There were so many pranks that we liked to pull on others in the house as well as on those in the fraternal and sorority system at our college. I remember one time we all awoke on a random Monday to find out that someone had broken into our house and did some innocent tar and feathering of certain pieces of artwork and photo composites throughout the main floor. We noticed that these same deranged criminals stole one of our beloved golden lions that stood on our front outdoor patio. That sumbitch was heavy. That took effort of multiple people. It only took a half day of gossip and connections to learn that the scoundrels were none other than the local sorority sisters that lived right down the road. As we made the demand to get our beloved Leo the Lion back, Zohan had already begun to formulate our revenge move on our fellow sisters.

When it came time to exact revenge, Zohan had a well laid out plan. He recruited me, another brother, and our good friend, Toolbox. Tool and Big Z were very close. Tool had pledged the year after I did. Tool came in blazing his Boston, Massachusetts bravado and outside voice. He was an absolute fit with the indigent crew of men who lived within our hallowed walls. Even if he was a bit outside the box, if you will. But he and Zohan hung out from the beginning.

Zohan gathered us all up in his 1969 Ford F-100. This thing was an absolute beast. We needed that beast to get where we were going. Zohan took us to the outskirts of Missoula. We are talking the hills leading up to the mountains. He was a man on a mission. When we finally traversed a whole field in typical Montana four-wheel drive fashion, Z jumped out of the truck and immediately opened the tailgate. He threw us each a shovel and told us to follow him. When we saw the large black garbage bags in his hands, we all kind of questioned whether this was going somewhere none of us wanted to go.

Thankfully, the shovels were simply to dig up some anthills. No dead body parts in this story. We all went at it and we dumped pounds of these ants in multiple garbage bags. Then we drove back towards town. When we got home, Zohan laid out the final parts of the plan. That night, around 3am, he would wake up a few select housemates and then we would follow him into the night and prepare the second stage of the plan. This consisted of borrowing a local port-a-potty on our walk down to our sisters' house. The five of us did all this without any hesitation or questioning of Big Z.

When we arrived at the large door of our sorority sisters' house, Zohan walked up to the huge front door with a Costco-sized honey bottle. He then proceeded to dump the entire contents of honey all over the front of the door. He then had us all throw the bags of swarming angry ants in the port-a-potty entrance. We opened the tops of each bag, then we slowly tipped the port-a-potty onto their front door, leaning it ever slightly so that the door of the port-a-potty was still shut. The bags of open ants were tilted with the potty. That poor, poor girl who happened to be the first one out the door the next morning. If only there had been security camera footage available in those golden days.

That's the kind of brother Zohan was. Never a dull moment. He had a strong long-term memory. He would hold out for months for retribution or to win at a prank war. He would also go the extra mile to protect or help any of his fraternity family. In fact, in the archives of USA Today, you will read about a brawl where most of the Montana Grizzly Football team came in like a wrecking crew to our neighboring fraternity and beat the hell out of many of those poor souls. Unbeknownst to the football team, it was really Zohan they were after. He attacked a football player who was kicked out of that neighboring fraternity's annual Woodstock party. That player then left to get a bunch of his teammates and returned to the scene of the crime. Zohan was nowhere to be found. Leave it to Zohan.

Now the crux of this story I am a bit ashamed to write about. It is the not true reflection of who I am today, as this was about as dumb as dumb gets. College is an interesting time of transformation and sketchy decision making.

So, my dumbass has a habit of seeing something I want, and making every effort to get it, whether it's a material object or an achievement goal. That's not the bad habit. The bad part was that back in the day I always took the easiest route to get what I wanted. This often involved putting on blinders to reality and common sense.

I always liked what I was driving. I was at that impressionable age where my car gave me confidence, which I then translated into my sexual prowess. I did say I was a dumbass in the paragraph above. When I saw the maroon Ford Probe GT on the used car dealer's lot, I knew I had to have it. What a great upgrade from the Nissan Sentra I was currently driving. It was speedy, sexy, and somewhat affordable on my monthly wages. I was sold. Not even thinking about the increase in car maintenance, gas prices, and insurance, I blindly went in to find out what it would take to get that car.

The used car lot was exactly what you would think. It smelled of wet cats and burnt hair in the negotiation trailer. That's when the very stand-up general manager came over to tell me what a great eye I had. The best car on his lot. However, there was something he had to disclose. The vehicle had a salvage title attached to it. Not knowing what that even meant, I went about getting the keys and taking that beauty out for a whirl. Seemed great to me as I was speeding off. I knew it was supposed to cost more. The similar cars I looked up in the bigger cities had much higher price tags. This thing would be mine.

Funny thing. My current credit union as well as a few of the bigger banks in town all turned me down. My credit was great. I had little to no debt. I was making good money for a college student. They all told me that because of the salvage title they were unable to help me secure financing for the car. Heartbroken, I told the dealer it was probably not going to happen right away. He told me to come back if I ever had enough cash to buy it. He would give me a discount.

Missoula is a funny town. Everyone truly knows you through only a few degrees of separation. What made it better for me was that I was waiting tables at one of the few restaurants in town. A well-known restaurant with plenty of local history. We did not yet have the franchise restaurants. So, I was doing well by working at one of the consistently busy places in town. It allowed me to me new people daily. Business leaders, police officers, bankers, and every other local occupation came through our restaurant. One of the people I met was a loan officer at one of the larger local banks in town. When I told her of my dilemma about buying my dream car, she handed me her card and told me to get a hold of her soon and she could help me out.

Two days later I was rolling around town in my new to me Ford Probe. That sumbitch was fast as hell and had an amazing stereo. I couldn't have been happier. I now could compete with my buddies because they all had razzle dazzle cars that their parents bought for them. I was living the dream. Until the higher gas bills, the higher insurance bills, and the routine maintenance started to roll in. Then that love turned to hate quick. It took me all of six months to realize what a stupid mistake I made. But lucky for me, I only had $500 cash down in the form of my previous car trade. Even better was when I started looking at trading it in, every dealership basically told me they would never take a salvage title car. I was stuck with that grand old Ford.

So about 9 months in, I started to think about what I could do to get rid of this car. It was draining my discretionary funds. Basically, the only way out of the car was for it to get totaled and then insurance would have to pay out on it. I had been in a few car wrecks prior to owning this car, so the thought crossed my mind that I would just wish to the world for it to get blindsided. I think I ran every uncontrolled intersection for two months straight. No luck. That bad boy was sticking with me.

Then one October night, I found myself in my buddy Zohan's basement room. He had moved himself down to the only room in the basement. He enjoyed being away from the noise and he was always bringing women back from the bars. He could do that in secrecy in that room. It was exactly what you would think a single basement room in an older fraternity would look like. One "sort of" conforming window in a concrete block. Dark, bleak, and perfect for Zohan.

As we passed around some beers and a Fireball bottle with the small group of brothers, the talk came to each other's cars. Zohan mentioned that he never had the chance to drive my Probe. He was always curious because he loved those Ford Probes. I told him he was welcome to it anytime, but make sure to not bring it back in one piece. He laughed and asked why. I told him about the salvage title issue and the fact it was bleeding me dry of discretionary funds. It took his brain about .03 seconds to come up with a solution. He told me with an absolute stoic face that I should leave the car on the street one night. He said that he had been in multiple wrecks with his beast Ford truck and barely had a dent to show for any of them. He said that if one night someone were to wreck into my car and then take off, who would ever know? Basically, he straight up offered to have his own version of demolition derby with my Probe problem.

I laughed it off. But I am not going to lie; it peaked my interest. Thankfully, the people in the dungeon room that night were too far gone to care about some dumb conversation that we had. I mostly forgot about the conversation too, but it did cross my mind a few times to clarify to big Z that we were just joking around. Life gets crazy and those couple of months were hectic and I never got the chance to say anything.

Imagine my surprise when my buddy and next-door neighbor in our fraternity house ran into my room at 4:30 AM one morning, shaking me violently out of my most likely post inebriated state. When I looked into the fierce eyes of a mad Irish man that I knew as Toolbox, I knew immediately something was very wrong. Funny how two wrongs make a right. Or something like that.

He proceeded to yell that my car had just been hit. And while he didn't have the perfect view of the crime, he did have a little brief sight of the culprit. He was telling me I had to come out front and quick. As I rushed out in only my boxer shorts, I barely noticed my roommates had awakened and were now part of the ruckus.

When I got outside, I was immediately aware of how little clothing I was wearing. I was also aware of my drunk Bostonian buddy leading me out to the front lawn. When he finally stopped, I saw why he was so excited. There, on the side of the road, was my mostly crumpled up Ford Probe. Well, at least a large majority of what was left of the left side of the car and the hood area. The pseudo car alarm I had installed was weakly wailing, a victim of a hard puncture to the horn system. Then it hit me like a ton of bricks. Fucking Zohan.

Toolbox was there to confirm my suspicions. He pulled me aside, which was a little awkward as I was only in my boxers and he was in a tank top and shorts. He had seen who hit my car. He wanted me to know that I should be careful what I told the responding officers. It was our good friend Zohan.

I wanted to just laugh. Laugh at the absurdity of the entire situation. As the police pulled up, they saw my skinny ass in only my boxers. Then they saw this crazy red headed bull next to me, only in his shirt and skivvies, at nearly 5 AM on fraternity row. I can see now how sometimes the stereotype is not too far off the mark. I told them I had no clue who it could have been. We lived on a main thoroughfare in a college district. Street parking was always full, and traffic was constant. This wasn't the first time some drunk asshole hit a car and took off. It has been happening for years.

As I went inside, Toolbox was very concerned I might have mentioned Zohan. I made sure he knew that I may have heard a rumor back in the day that my car had a hit out on it. I told him to not worry.

Of course, it was Zohan.

As Toolbox and I sat taking a shot of whiskey at 7 AM we just stared at Zohan. He was in the spirit world. No, he was not dead, but his brain was taking a metaphysical vacation. He told us he had consumed a cap from a magic mushroom, then started drinking some whiskey, His wall had spoken to him and told him that it was time to wreck Chance's car. And then he did just that. And then drove to his girlfriend's place until we went to work. Here were Toolbox and I listening to the most interesting story of the night. Still in our boxers and Z in his white tee. Good times at the fraternity.

The real joke of this story?

My now completely wrecked Probe was towed away to a local junkyard. As was protocol, my insurance company, which is now defunct, had to send an adjuster to look over the damage and make an assessment. And as Karma goes, the miracle of the week happened that day. The car was fixable above the total loss zone. So, for the $500 deductible I would get some new paneling, new lights, and a brand-new security system. My car would be as good as new. I was even able to keep the salvage title along with it.

#FML

I owe a quick apology to my parents. I had no idea that Zohan would go this crazy. Just like I had no idea about George stealing all your alcohol and hiding his beer in our garage. Random. Of course, I feel badly about lying, but mostly I am sorry for the $500 deductible that Zohan made you pay to get my precious gem of a bad decision out of the body shop. My bad.

Casa Bonita!!!

When we made it to the Brown Palace in the heart of downtown Denver, we were elated. My wife and I were officially moving back much closer to our families. We were also starting a new chapter in our lives. We were leaving our current home in northern California and heading for the wild west of Colorado. We were in Denver on a weekend scouting trip to find a place to live.

The company I was working for had been recently acquired by a giant corporation. As was often the case, our staff and assets were just things to be acquired. We were the expendables. I knew that the branch I was running in Sacramento was probably on the chopping block, so it created an opportunity for my wife and I to carve out our next adventure.

When I told my wife that we had a shot at doing this, she was a little hesitant. Ava was working for a great school district and loved her job, but the dynamics of dealing with the politics and law of her position were taxing. When she asked me where I was thinking of moving, I knew her mind had drifted with mine and saw an exciting opportunity around the corner.

I told her my first option out of northern California would be to just move down south to San Diego. She was immediately in agreement but there were a couple of drawbacks. Next, I told her I wanted to also move to Denver. This she wanted to hear more about. It was much closer to both of our families and even though she hadn't been through Denver since she was with me, driving up the I-25, she had heard good things about the city. Although the thought of going back to sub-zero days in January and up to twelve feet of snow in March was a little daunting compared to sunny southern California. She was absolutely perplexed with my third suggestion.

"You haven't even ever been to Austin" was her correct response.

It wasn't the fact that I had not been to Austin yet, it was the fact that it was even in play as it was very out of context. I assured her that even though I had never been to Austin I knew it was like San Diego and Denver. We would be well suited for any of those choices, except we would be a little more strapped because of San Diego's home pricing compared to where we were coming from. When I finally got to visit Austin many years later, I was pleased to find out my assumptions about that fair city were well placed and all correct.

When we finally deciphered all our wants and needs with each other, the shining star was Denver. It made a ton of sense and we were pining to get back to a place that would have all four seasons within the calendar year. Our family being closer was just icing on top. How little did we know that quite a few of our friends would come to find the awesomeness of Denver in their own, unconnected way? One set of those friends happened to also be looking to move there from California, just from southern California. Burbank to be exact.

As it worked out, I contacted the manager of the branch that controlled my position in Denver. I knew the manager through mutual friends in the company and he knew me through some of the same channels and through my reputation within our company. As the world generally works for me in certain situations, it just so happened that when I called Kevin, he told me they had been looking for a rep for Denver and that if I wanted the open position then I could have it. No interview. No corporate internal docs. Even though we had just been acquired by one of the nation's largest banks. Within minutes of introducing myself I had accepted the job and was very happy to tell my wife that we would be moving to beautiful Colorado. She was beyond happy. Her patience had worn thin with her current position and NorCal in general. She wanted a change as much as I did.

Now we had to jump into a full-on sprint. Kevin wanted me in Colorado in a couple of months. So now not only did I have to break the news to my current boss at the time, I also had to figure out how to sell our home in winter and in two months. I didn't even blink twice as I knew that between my wife and me, it would all work out.

My boss at that time had not only become a mentor to me, but he and his family had become family to us. We struggled through business pains and persevered, but we also had a great time when we were away from our hectic work schedules. I was a little relieved when he didn't throw me out the front bay window of his office. He was sad to have me leave but in his true stoic nature he was very happy for my wife and me to be closer to home and to be happy on a new adventure. He begrudgingly agreed to my transfer and told me that someday we would be back to working with each other. He was right.

With the transfer approved and the house on the market, our next move was to get to Denver and figure out where to live. Ava had been to Colorado back in high school and I had only driven by downtown on the

25. It was time to spread our wings, so we found a local celebrity realtor and booked some showings with her.

Only in California. Well, there are a few markets that will fit the next statement, but fucking California takes the cake. The day we were scheduled to leave Sacramento we got a call from our realtor. We had an offer coming in. We had the damn house on the market for just over 48 hours. Right on cue as we were getting ready to leave, we got the good news. The offer was legit, and it was $10,000 over our asking price. Getting offers over the asking price was not unheard of during this time. Even in NorCal, the area was exploding and there was not enough inventory to supply the demand. We were delighted. We could get to Denver with a clean slate and be able to live how we really wanted to. It was incredibly cheaper than California. We signed off on the offer and went on to the airport with an incredible weight off our shoulders. California had worked out perfectly the six years we visited her.

Then the bad news came.

As we were getting ready to board our flight to Denver, we got a phone call from our real estate agent. She had some bad news. As quick as the offer came, it went away just as quick. The potential buyer had apparently spoke to his wife after he signed the offer and that didn't go over so well. So, well within his legal rights, he canceled the contract. We tried our hardest to not let it get us down and ruin our fun trip. Besides finding a place to live, we had three days to explore our next home. So, we boarded the flight and immediately ordered a couple of Vodka sodas.

Fucking California. I can't even make this shit up. Buyers and sellers of real estate in the majority of California will absolutely understand the below process of buying and selling a home in a hot California market.

We had just landed in east Nebraska. Also known by its other name: Denver International Airport, DIA for short. The mountains of western Colorado seemed very far away. By the time the half hour train ride to baggage claim had stopped, the 2G service to my Motorola V3 flip phone had just kicked in. We both had messages. We grabbed our bags and pulled up the voicemail as it was from our realtor. She was overjoyed. In the two-hour flight from Sacramento to Denver, she had sold our home. Again. She also got us a better offer as she technically could tell the buyer that we were reviewing other offers. This one stuck. The buyers happened to have their daughter and son in law in the housing community and they wanted to be close to the grandkids. They were making a ton of money off their home in Santa Barbara so the over the asking price they paid was understandable to them. I really can't describe the elation of that process. We knew it was a onetime deal and we would never get that to happen again, but we were relishing in the afterglow of selling our house, losing the sale, then selling the home again in less than three hours. All docs were signed that night. Without hesitation.

As we left DIA in a state of renewed bliss, we were concerned. Why was the airport 40 some miles away from civilization? We were literally driving through wheat fields to get to downtown Denver. As soon as we saw the high rises in the background all concerns were erased. The mountains were close and the fresh drift of snow on the ground felt warm and welcoming.

When we pulled off on the Broadway exit that our printed-out MapQuest was showing us, we started to get concerned again. This was a weird industrial part of northern Denver with a lot of burned out and condemned buildings. We were not meeting our realtor until the next day, but we wanted to scope out the downtown area where we were looking. In fact, that night we were booked at one of Denver's oldest operating hotels, the Brown Palace. Everything in the area where we were looking at places as well as where we were staying all looked awesome in the pictures online. Once again, like our first trip into California, we were seeing different real estate then advertised. Still happy though.

We got within a few blocks of the general area we would be looking at in the next few days and sighed a huge breath of relief. The downtown area was as advertised. We had just driven in an unusual way to get there. What we thought was odd was the block that we decided to park on and then hoof it around the lower downtown area was void of cars. What was even more weird was the fact that every parking meter had a yellow hood over the pay and timer part. We weren't sure that we could park there but then a truck pulled in and parked in front of one of these masked meters. We said, "fuck it" and parked. At worse we would get a ticket.

As I got out of the car and looked at my wife who was examining the hooded meter, I heard a scream. That scream repeated itself and seemed to get louder. My wife also noticed it. I looked to my right and saw this woman, at the far end of this block, waving her arms frantically in our direction and absolutely screaming at us. Then she started running towards us. Literally our first visit into our new home seemed to be starting out as something from a horror movie.

As the woman got closer to us, I could see she was older, probably in her mid to late fifties. My wife and I were concerned as to why she was running over to us. As she caught her breath, she said she had seen my wife looking at the yellow hood and trying to pull it off to possibly pay. We told her we had never seen anything like it, and it was our first visit to Denver proper. She made sure to welcome us to Denver, then she laughed. She said that it was a holiday weekend and that the parking downtown was free. Right then and there my wife and I looked at each other with an understanding glance. We knew we were home.

After a brief walk around LoDo, it was time to check into our fancy hotel and then figure out where to grab some grub for the night. At this point in our lives, we didn't really have a lot of experience with upscale hotels. We wanted to experience that pleasure on this trip. The Brown Palace did not disappoint. At all. As the bellhop was carting up our luggage to our suite, my cell started vibrating in my pocket. I saw it was my buddy Glen. He asked me where I was. We hadn't chatted in a few weeks as he had been traveling for his company, Absolute Poke. He had just gotten back from Costa Rica. I told him that the wife and I got a quick ok to travel to Denver to check out our future home. He just laughed. I think he said, "Only you dude". I told him briefly about the quick job transfer and he laughed again. He then told me that he and his wife were less than a mile away from us. His job was changing up and his wife had just decided to buy a company that was based out of Denver. They also were on a last-minute trip to find new digs. So random, but so my life.

I told him to get their ass over to our hotel to grab some drinks and figure out a good place to eat. We were still in the infancy stages of cell service and smartphones were a thing of the distant future. No Yelp or "look for" food in this area. Nope, good old Yellow Pages and concierge. Glen told me that our mutual friend, Barney, had been to Denver many times. He was going to call him and get his recommendations.

As we waited for our surprise friends to arrive, we perused the hotel guide just to see what the area was like. Lower Downtown Denver was still growing and transitioning. It still had its drug addiction and homeless issues throughout the area, but for the most part the young money was moving in and gentrification was afoot. There were plenty of steak houses, Mexican cuisine, even some sushi joints very near our hotel. There had to be some fantastic restaurants for us to try.

When Glen and his wife knocked on our door, we were more than ready to head out. They had a cab drop them off as they were staying a longer distance than a walk. It was January and damn cold out especially since they were coming from SoCal. Even us in NorCal had to get used to the new cold. Loved every bit of it. I told them I had looked around at some of the eating options and we had plenty to choose from. Glen was having none of it. He told me he had spoken to Barney and he knew exactly where we were all going, some place called Casa Bonita. An exotic Mexican cuisine restaurant that was tucked away in an up and coming part of Denver.

Some of you are dying laughing right now. Some of you are calling us names. Others are thinking that they have heard that name somewhere, but they can't quite put their finger on it. Let me help you out. Ever watch South Park? Did you ever watch the episode about Cartman freaking out because he was going to a "special" restaurant for his birthday? Yeah, that episode, aptly titled "Casa Bonita" is probably what you are remembering. Let me tell you, Trey and Matt nailed everything about it.

As the four of us were piling in the cab, I asked Glen why he thought we needed to drive out of downtown Denver to eat at this place when there were so many great restaurants within walking distance. He told me that Barney was so excited that the four of us were in Denver together and that he had such fond memories of this restaurant. It was a hidden gem that not many people knew about. He was insistent that we all go there at least once this weekend. Glen was a sucker for enthusiasm. Fell for it, hook, line and sinker. That should have been our first clue something was amiss. I even remember thinking to myself that something was suspect. But Ava and I were in a great mood and we were with friends, what could be the worst thing that could happen?

The second clue should have been the cab driver's facial expression when we told him where we were headed. Like a good cab driver, he turned around with his hidden smile and told us we would be there in about 20 minutes. For the four of us, coming from the traffic congestion mecca of the world, the fact that we were driving 15 or so miles and getting there in 20 minutes was a miracle.

The third clue we all should have realized was that even though we were talking amongst each other in the cab, we all noticed the legendary Colfax Avenue we were taking to get to Casa Bonita. Every block after the Broncos Stadium seemed to get worse. There were cops about every block, some just sitting on the road in their cars, some were throwing shifty looking characters on their hoods. Pawn shops, hourly motels, super used car dealerships, and one old broken down Target they were getting ready to implode, all greeted us out the windows of our cab. So really a bunch of clues that should have told us we had been duped.

Finally, the cab driver told us we were turning into the shopping mall for our destination. There it was. Just like they portrayed it in that South Park episode. Right in the middle of a rundown strip mall, with a Payday Loan store to the right of it, was the 30-foot-tall pink steeple and giant pink fountain that announced the entrance to the famed Casa Bonita. The good news was that even though my wife and I wanted to strangle Glen right there in the cab, we didn't have to do shit. Glen's wife mumbled a couple of words and gave Glen the world's worst death stare. We had seen it plenty of times before. This was the "no sex for a couple of months" type of stare.

We had no choice. We paid the driver fifty bucks and slowly walked to the entrance in disbelief. What greeted us next was straight out of third grade. A set of chains that weaved the customer to the front of the ordering line. It was a fucking hot lunch line from the 80s. This is where you ordered your food. I would call the food a mix of third world Taco Bell meets those dry rations you get in the military for survival. Just add water. What could we do? We still had some sort of hope that there was something behind the ordering line, the promised front row seating, that was going to make up for all of this.

After we ordered from the five menu options available, we were led to the back room where our table would be. What we saw was beyond belief. We entered another dimension. We saw a huge cliff in front of us, and we saw a couple of people at the top of the cliff yelling out into the open restaurant while sword fighting. Then one of the actors yelled and fell about 30 feet to the bottom of the cliff. To our amusement, there was a huge pool at the bottom. This was the legendary Casa Bonita. Legendary might be stretching it a bit. This was their schtick. The food was known to be what it was, but their nightly live entertainment was where it was at. If you were under the age of eight. This was not a "first night" in your new city type of experience.

As we quickly raised our flag at our dinner table to let the waitress know we needed unlimited refills of their incredibly sugared strawberry margaritas, we all turned our attention to Glen. He could tell he was in trouble with the crowd. He simply told us that he should have not trusted Barney and his judgement was clouded by the three or four whiskeys he drank before he spoke with him.

We could not finish quickly enough. Even though we ended up staying until they closed shop, it still took another hour for our cab to show up. Why? Because we were in the middle of one of the most notoriously shit areas of Denver at that time. No cab driver wanted that assignment as there was always a risk of death. By the time the cab finally appeared, we were all done. No extra late night for any of us. We did have a call to make though.

The absolute knowledge of getting screwed over by one of your buddies is undeniable. Pretty sure every single reader here can acknowledge that. When Barney answered his cell at almost midnight his time, he knew we knew. As we were all aggressively yelling at him on why the fuck he recommended that spot we could barely hear his answer between his guttural laughing. He said he knew exactly what he had told Glen and that he used Glen's need for five-star recommendations against him. He said Glen also failed to ask the ultimate question. Barney had not been to Denver since he was eight. His last experience that he remembered in Denver was way back in the day when his mom and dad took him to Casa Bonita. Had Glen asked the simple question of when Barney was last in Denver, he probably would have told him and that would have ended our hundred-dollar, round trip taxi out to the ghetto of Denver.

The four of us still hold that story dear for many reasons. We have never inflicted that same pain onto any of our friends, even though the enjoyment would be immense. I still lie in wait though. The payback to Barney will be beyond comparison. I have thought about the day of reckoning for close to thirteen years now. Someday I might just share with you all how that finally goes.

I also had Barney sign an agreement. The only agreement I needed in this book. You see, I know that once he reads this story, the joy of what he did to his friends and their wives will uncontrollably take over his body and he might just have a heart attack as his body and heart have aged like a fine wine. I do not want his death on my hands because of something he successfully pulled off many, many years ago.

*Day Jah Foo : The overwhelming feeling that you have heard
this shit before.* ~ Anonymous

BREAKFAST IN VEGAS

I owe a lot of gratitude to the TV series Friends. It not only entertained the fuck out of me, it also gave my wife and me an opportunity to bond outside of the usual partying and mayhem in our sorority and fraternity lives. It also gave me some seriously great ideas for messing with my own friends. Art does influence life.

The six of us were fresh out of college and even though we all had gone separate ways geographically, we still all kept in touch. We tried to arrange weekends where the guys could get together and catch up. Theses sporadic weekends were magical times. They were always chaotic and full of immature fun. We all had real adult jobs and were trying hard to be mature. I was the only married one of this motley group. Chris had finalized his first divorce.

It didn't matter. We all loved these trips. Well, most of us. Some of the crew was tired of the constant stupidity that came with these guys' trips. Our destination? Las Vegas, of course. George and I decided to arrive a day early to begin the mini reunion. The others had work obligations or travel limits and could not partake in our start. Plus, most of them thought three days in Vegas were more than enough. George and I did not agree.

Our first day was great. Nothing out of control, just some catching up and retelling of our crazy life stories. We even managed to win some cash from gambling that covered our food and drink bills and put a little something in our pocket. Of course, as always in Vegas, we should have stopped gambling. As usual by the end of the trip we would all be in the hole. Some way worse off than others.

When George and I stumbled back to our room at the Excalibur, we relished the fact that we each would get our own bed. We only had two queen beds, tomorrow we would have to figure out where to stick everyone else. Hopefully, two on the foldout couch or floor. The plus would be that Chris and Murray usually ended up finding someone of the opposite sex, and usually ended up over at that person's residence. Sadly, this was standard operating procedure for this crew in the early stages of our group trips. We all knew we wanted to spend our allocated money on other amenities like entertainment and gambling.

The next morning, we were awoken by the arrival of Murray and Frank. They had both been pregaming on the flight. George and I were up and dressed in no time and headed out to our next adventure. This was the time that the Vegas strip was growing up and making the huge transition to what it is now. The MGM and, the just built, New York, New York were the hot hotels. The other side of the strip was still in its older, original glory. We started drinking and gambling right away. By the time we realized it was mid-day we looked up to find ourselves down near Caesars. We knew it was time to get back to the hotel to meet our other buddies.

As we pulled our vampires asses out of the casino, we all winced at the brightness of the afternoon sun. George was a little antsy as we crossed the walkway to the other side of the strip. We thought it was because he was super happy that he was still up on the gambling wins on his second day. He wanted to jump into the little margarita joint that was at the corner of the walkway. We told him we needed to walk the mile or so back to our hotel so that we were not late meeting the last of the crew. We had rudimentary cell phones and limited service on those shitty cell plans. George didn't care, he was on a mission. His day and a half of abuse on his body was kicking in. He needed a shitter and he needed it quick. We all laughed and told him to find one fast. We grabbed a drink for the road and waited out his explosive episode. Unfortunately, the small joint did not allow tourists to use their amenities, so out ran George and told us we had to take the walkway back to the hotel across the street. We politely told him that we needed to head in the direction of our hotel, no backtracking. He told us to wait right there and that he would be back in a flash.

We did not want to wait for George, but we finally agreed to find something to do while we waited. We watched him awkwardly stumble up the stairs to the walkway. When we watched him stop and stand at the beginning of the slow-moving walkway, we decided we were not waiting for him. The moving walkway would take him ten minutes to get to the front of the hotel then another 15 or more minutes to find his rest room and get back. We needed to move on to meet Chris and Dick. Looking back, we should have waited for him. One of us could have stayed behind to wait out George's alien reveal ceremony, but we were all in our zone and not thinking at our best level.

We met up with the rest of the party just as they were getting out of their cab. Pleasantries were exchanged and then we all headed up to our shared tiny room. Dick and Chris quickly settled in and asked why we were a man short. We explained George's predicament. They said they would have bounced also. Besides, we had told George we were heading back to our hotel so he should have been right behind us. We all headed down to the main bar to wait for George.

About an hour later we all realized that none of us had heard from George. We went back up to the room to check, but he had not been there. We left him a note that we were all heading to our dinner reservation and that he needed to change and meet us there. We figured the internal organ surgery that he explored in the restroom might have taken a different route. Would not be the first time. The real probability was that he got involved in a raucous game of craps. He was an addicted gambler back then. He was known to spend hours at a time on his "hot hand" tables. Like me, George has never met a stranger. At this time, we had no idea where he was, but figured Vegas was small enough and he had our cell numbers. He would find us when he was ready.

George was pissed. Like sixth grade, you stole my extra guys in the video game Contra, pissed. He couldn't believe that when he meandered back to the spot, he had left us at, that we were not still there waiting upon his important arrival. He quickly searched neighboring casinos looking for any sign of us but did not have any luck. He was also inebriated enough to not look at his cell and see that we had texted him to meet us back at the hotel. He walked down the south strip in a huff and decided two things were going to happen. First, he would call his mother to buy him a plane ticket out of Vegas that night. If we left him, then he didn't need us. Second, he was going to blow his four-day allotment at the tables in the next hour while his mom booked his flight back to Rancho Cucamonga. He was 24 years old.

He ended up across the street at the MGM. He found the perfect shrimp cocktail section of the cigar bar and he bellied up and called his mom. Sadly, for George, his mom was done with his shit. When she told him to think about what he was asking her to do. She told him he should sleep off the booze and maybe reevaluate things in the morning. He angrily hung up on his sweet mother. He did realize that he could probably call the airlines himself, but then after another Gibson he was back to being mad again. He headed over to the hotel to confront the group and break up with us all right then and there. I mean we had only known each other since we were 7 years old. This was his straw breaking the back moment. Again, sadly for George, he was met with disappointment. When he stormed into the room ready to hit the first person he saw, he was met with blackness. No one was around. He still had not checked his texts. One more whiskey water was enough to make him rent a hotel entertainment video and put himself to sleep. His ex-buddies were all going to pay for that in-room video purchase, he told himself before drifting off to blackout land.

When the rest of us showed up around 2 AM slightly concerned that we had not seen our good buddy in about eight hours, we were met with some relief. George's usual Halloween horror tape sounds were emitting from under his blanket. We knew he was safe. As Frank rolled him over to ask where the hell he had been, George made it clear through his nonverbal grunts that he was extremely mad at each and every one of us. We all fell asleep too quickly to really care.

After some self-realizations, George was understandably embarrassed at some of his actions from the prior night. When he heard our side of the story and then told his side of the story, the combined laughter in the room probably woke up our hotel neighbors. Everything was quickly forgiven, and we vowed for a night of debauchery as a group on our final night together. Chris was only in town for the day and a half and hadn't seen George since he arrived the night prior. We made reservations at a nice steak house. That's when George realized he was now down a grand for his last three days. The gambling fairies were not as good to him as they were on our first night. So back to the races we went.

By the time we made it to dinner we were all back to being best friends and the real party was starting. Around the time we were delivered the check, half of the table thought it would be awesome to take a cab out of town. They really wanted to visit the couple of legal brothels that were near Vegas. The other half of us were considering going to the higher end bars and keeping the memory train rolling. By the time the bill was settled, so was our group. George, Frank, and Dick were calling a cab to take them out of town. Murray, Chris, and I decided to pass on that amazing idea and go back to the strip. While there was some trash talking and guilt tripping, we said goodnight and wished each other well. That's how we parted that fateful night.

The events of that night could not have gone more differently. The three of us who ended up on the strip made it to a couple different venues, each one getting better and more packed. Enough to keep us distracted until close to 1 AM, which is when we called it a night. The three of us hopped in a cab and headed back to the hotel. Chris and I had unnaturally early flights the next morning, we were already going to be sleep deprived. We literally had less than five hours until we had to head to the airport. Murray was tracking one of his legendary migraines. He knew he had one too many Bud Lights. When we pulled up to the hotel, there was commotion in the cab ahead of us. Sure enough, George and Frank piled out of the cab. Both were holding half full suitcases of beer. When they saw us, Frank ran over with the renewed energy of a 12-year-old. He had an amazing story to share with us. Chris and Murray told them that they were done. The story could wait for another day. Which is also where I will leave off. Not my story to tell or even share. Maybe some other time.

I wasn't done. I reasoned with my inner self that I could catch some much-needed Z's on the ride home in a few hours. I wanted to hear their adventures and I was still ahead on my gambling. I wanted to press my luck and George and Frank were in the same boat. So away we went to a blackjack table that would hold the three of us.

A half an hour later we were waiting in line to grab some much-needed breakfast as it was also the last of our dumbass' reserve money. I was now down $500 for the weekend, Frank was down a cool $1500, and George was down a lot more. Plus, he had a super awkward conversation with his mom to look forward to when he called her back.

By the time the two of them plastered together their drunk antics from the past six hours, I was rolling on the booth. The day had done them in. It was now almost three in the morning and they had faded. Right after they ordered their three meals (each) they decided it was best to take a snooze. Next to me, in the booth. Frank was out first. George was just resting his eyes here and there.

I am man of opportunity. While many people have different definitions of opportunity. I usually make it what it needs to be in the moment. I asked our wonderful waitress if she could help a friend out and find me a black sharpie. She glanced over at Frank's tilted head and bulldog snorts coming out of his mouth and knew exactly what I was thinking.

When she brought me back the sharpie, Frank had woken himself up a couple of times looking for his meals. George was gone. At least George's legendary snores were to a minimum. When I had a brief glimpse of opportunity, I uncapped the sharpie and started my masterpiece of art on

Frank. Frank's internal alarm was buzzing. He woke up right away and caught me red handed. This was not my first go around with a Sharpie around him. Before he could break into his well-deserved angry dissertation toward me, I threw my finger up to my lips and shouldered in George's direction. His anger turned quickly into childhood delight as he saw George was right in between us and had found a great pillow in the bench behind us. Fully exposing his Amish tan for anyone in possession of a black marker.

The waitress helped us out and found another Sharpie. To our credit, Frank and I did try to wake up George to tell him the food had finally come. I also want to go on public record and say that I also literally told George that if he did not wake up, I was going to introduce his face to some beautiful face art.

Frank and I quickly went to work. Let me paint a picture. Frank and I, like most of America, were faithful weekly viewers of Friends. In one of the later episodes in their 10 seasons was a hilarious episode where Ross had gone to Vegas only to end up in one of his usual idiotic decisions. He also became very inebriated and Rachel drew on his face. She drew whiskers, painted his nose black, and put his name on his forehead. He then walked through the casino floor and interacted with random strangers with plenty of laughs. We decided at breakfast that we would recreate that same artwork and set the same type of scene. His whiskers were long enough for everyone but him to see. His nose was too hard to see. But instead of his name across his forehead we spelled out MEOW.

George was groggy but super excited that his triple bacon and cheese omelet with extra sausage gravy had arrived. He glared over at us and asked Frank why he was laughing. Frank made up some stupid story about laughing at a bachelor party that wandered past our table. George grunted and headed back to his healthy portioned meal. That's when the real fun began.

The inside jokes between Frank, myself, and our waitress were priceless. We all would make some sort of mention about something to do with cats. Our waitress dropped the mother of all jokes though. She asked George if had ever seen the musical Cats. It was in Vegas at the time. George was smitten. He knew this lovely waitress was taken by his manly charm and even more manly appetite. He told her that he hadn't but that if she wanted to go, he would gladly take her. I think that's when Frank snorted water out of his nose. He was always one laugh away from making George aware of his hidden artwork. It was time to go before he blew it for the rest of the world.

We told George that breakfast was on us. A sort of "sorry" for the hardships he experienced over the last 48 hours. We were very happy his mom had not flown his dumbass home. The trip wouldn't be the same without him. Especially these final hours together. Happy with his gut full, and even happier he had a 40-minute cat nap, he fully bounced back at nearly 4 AM.

As we were leaving the restaurant, we bumped into a small bachelorette party that was coming in to get their grub on. I happened to be behind George, so when I saw these ladies' drunken eyes focus in a squint on George I quickly intercepted. I gave them the universal "shh" finger to my lips and told them that we too were in town to celebrate our friend's future nuptials. Which was only a half lie. They didn't need to know that he wouldn't get married for another 18 or so years. I gave George a wink and introduced him by his nickname "Kitty Cat". Because he was as sweet as a kitten but manly like a lion. Thankfully this group of young ladies were all about being in on the joke. They immediately started catcalling George and giving him the "meowwwww" whisper.

George was in absolute heaven. Not only did the cute waitress just ask him out on a date (in his head), but now this group of lovely ladies were all focused on him. Just him. This was making up for his very large loss of funds that he deposited into the Vegas casinos. It was also making up for the debacle at the Cathouse earlier that evening. Things were looking up for George. Now, I am not sure what prompted his next actions, but those actions were glorious.

He was all about being playful with his new group of admirers. So, he decided that he would act like a cat. Yup. He started meowing back at them and started to do air claws towards them. He even did a little lick on one of his imaginary paws and then wet back his hair. The girls were dying laughing. So was Frank. He was doubled over the steel gate and laughing in uncontrollable fashion. I really thought this was going to tip off George. Nope. He was enamored that so many women found him irresistible that night. We had to move on.

At this point I needed to leave with Chris to get to our flights on time. We dragged George out of the restaurant. He was considering getting another meal and flirting with his new friends. They gave him some last meows back and it was time to trek across the casino floor to our elevator. This next part was 100% just like Friends. George was in happy go lucky spirits and thought that everyone needed to see his cat routine. To his surprise they all laughed and gave him high fives or hugs. This was the life George had left back home in Montana. He was back at being the best bartender in the world at the best bar in Montana. But he didn't know a soul that he was interacting with on his trip back to our room.

When we made it back to our room, it was my time to leave. While George was on cloud nine now, he would turn into Mr. Hyde when he found out we had messed with him. I did not want anything to do with that. When we busted through the room, we found Chris and Dick fast asleep. No sign of Murray. We figured he found a little side action and was out. Chris pried his eyes open. I pulled him close and whispered that we had a half an hour to get to the airport and I also mentioned for him to shut the fuck up when he saw George's new tattoos. He was confused until the lights came on and George was there to give him a hug goodbye. Chris was now entering a sober zone, so he knew the implications of mentioning anything about George's artwork. They hugged it out, George gave him a kitty cat paw and pounced on his open bed spot.

As I said goodbye to all who were up and conscious, I just had a memory of walking past the bathroom and hearing the oddest sounds. It sounded like a baby seal that was in dire stress. Very odd. I also heard Frank trying to suppress his laughs and George continuing to meow at him.

When I got off the plane about three hours after I left Vegas, I had a new voicemail. I knew who it would be from. I wish that I could save those old voicemails so that I could share with you the absolute anger that I heard in George's voice. While I couldn't understand half of what he was yelling into the message, I did pick up that he had discovered his artwork and the next time he saw me he was going to do unpleasant and very unmentionable things to my wellbeing. Thankfully for me it would be a few months, and many therapeutic conversations with George, before we were physically reunited. I blamed the majority on Frank. Of course.

The best part about this story happened when George and I finally got together. He told me how everything unfolded, including his inner monologue rage. Right after Chris and I had headed out of the room he needed to release the demons that he had just scarfed down. As he entered the larger bathroom, he tried to be respectful and not turn on the light as to not disturb the people sleeping. As he sat himself on the toilet, he said he heard something coming from the shower area that did not sound human. It was like a groaning but with a bit of creepy weeping. He could only describe the sound as something he once heard in a movie he had watched. That movie was the Crying Game. The scene that unfolded was just as unique.

He switched the light on and opened the shower. There was Murray, huddled up in nothing but his Marine tighty whities, sopping wet from a recent shower. He was in the fetal position rocking and groaning. Apparently, Murray had a hidden allergy to something that was in Bud Light. It gave him massive migraines and this behavior is what helped him get through those tough episodes. George simply asked if everything was ok, and if Murray needed any medical attention. Murray said he did not, but that if George could turn the shower back on absolute cold, he would be mighty appreciative.

It was during that cold shower that Murray got his surprise. He heard George yell about as loud as he had ever heard him. So much so that it reignited Murray' migraine that was almost gone. He didn't have the energy to see if George had fallen in the toilet or what was going on. He would later see the artwork that George was trying his hardest to scrub off.

One of the largest triggers that made George leave me that death threat on my voicemail was the fact that after he had turned on the shower for Crying Game, he saw the whiskers. When he saw the black nose and when he read "Meow" on his forehead he flashed back to the last two hours at breakfast and going through the casino. Every single interaction and conversation, all related to cats came rushing back in his memory. It was then he realized that I had already left, and he could not inflict immense pain upon me or Frank. The anger was warranted. The time between visits would help the veiled death threats subside.

He still can't watch that episode of Friends though. The PTSD is real for him.

WATERED DOWN EXPECTATIONS

Them lies a line in the sand. For each of us, that line is a summation of our tipping points. The point where we lose control of our normal functions and cease to exist in the world that we are accustomed to. Sometimes that point can be reached on a normal day, sometimes outside influencing factors play a large part of the break down. My poor friend Barney found out the hard way where his breaking point was.

It was the mid-nineties. This was awkward transition in American culture, and it was an even more awkward transition within our fraternity. We were slowly declining. The house was literally falling apart and our limited knowledge we gained from our fathers about fixing shit was not helping. The sororities around us we still doing well, but for some reason the fraternities just could not find their groove. New members were down across the board. The population at our University was also starting to decline. When we elected Barney as our new fraternity president, we thought we would finally see some changes. He was great with social relations and he also was able to wrangle the politics with our national leaders. A perfect fit to lead the next generation of house members to a more successful and fruitful future existence.

Barney was one of the first people in house that I did not know from high school, but I immediately took a liking to him. Not only did Barney sell power tools at Sears to my father, he had also assimilated to our very close group of hometown friends. Plus, he drove a 1985 VW Jetta that had no floorboards in the passenger side. He engineered a cardboard box contraption that kept out the road noise while he drove the 345 one-way trip from Billings to Missoula. The guy was interesting. The day I entered his new President's room apartment I noticed a standing globe and a wine rack full of twelve different wines. The other 25 members living within the walls of the fraternity could maybe count one bottle of wine between all of us. That might be stretching it.

When Barney decided to not go back home for winter break and stick around with the five local guys staying in the very empty house, we knew it was going to be a fun week. George, I, and a few other guys were around working our various jobs. Barney had to work weird shifts at Sears, but he was happy to be around as the new leader of this odd crew.

We had a massive snow drop that winter break. One of the nights it snowed almost 36 inches. We got snowed in at our house. Well, we did the best shoveling we could, but most of us were not going anywhere. Lucky for us one of our Chicago brothers, aptly nicknamed Jake the Snake, was also snowed in with us. Also awesome was that Jake was in a stellar and sharing mood. Which was nice because when our beer ran out, and we were down to hard alcohol, Jake mentioned that he had something that could change up the drinking game. He had somehow come across an ounce or so of some green herb. Some Mary Jane. A little Sticky. But it was Montana, so more like wilted flowers in a cinnamon flowerbed. Regardless, it gave us a way of getting through the blizzard of 1996.

There were only six of us stuck in that 10,000 square foot home. We all had our different interests, but we all enjoyed each other's company. So, it was not weird when Barney showed up at my second story room out of the blue. What was a little odd, was that Jake showed up seconds, just after Barney. Jake was a happy go lucky dude, but he generally didn't socialize with us. We all sat there together for a moment in a winter blizzard bliss and then Jake produced a happy hour product that could only be described as burnt grass from last season's late prairie grass fire. Barney and I were game, though.

It was a bad choice for one of the three of us.

When Jake left the room, I remember staring at Barney, wondering why he was in my room. He simply told me that because I had the best stereo system in the house, he needed my help. I happily obliged. He told me that his sister's birthday was coming up and that he wanted to make an awesome mixtape for her. Something that would move her. I told him that I had made multiple mixtapes for random people off this stereo and that I would be glad to help for a couple hours.

To this day I feel sorry for his sister. Not that she did bad in life, or that she hated that mixtape (probably), but mainly because I remember what we put on that special mix. We are talking everything from Phil Collins', "In the Air Tonight" to "No Diggity" from Blackstreet (ft. Dr Dre). That poor sister never stood a chance.

I can remember about two hours later that Barney played the "A" side of the mixtape we were crafting. We had somehow managed to overlay the same song for the entire first side. Not on purpose, it was just the way it worked out. We had to replace Janet Jackson's "Pleasure Principle" with many different songs. That mixtape took four hours. That's really what I want Barney's sister to know.

The best part about finishing that mixtape was that during the recording I had great conversations with Barney. We already knew each other but this was something on a different level. Honestly the main thing I remember is that I had an amazing time trying to figure out at the end of each song which one to put next.

What was even more strange was what happened after the recording session. Jake stopped back by just to see how we were doing. Apparently, we were not doing well enough. So, Jake broke out his special stash of Mary Jane and forced us to partake with him. Which helped zero in Barney's situation. He was already tipsy on a bottle or two of red wine.

When he stumbled into my room demanding the mixtape that we had just completed, I knew it was my semi sworn duty to fuck with him. I was not nearly in as bad as shape as my buddy. I told him to take a seat and we would put in the tape and make sure it was what he wanted to give his sister. He was infatuated with the PlayStation game I was playing, Resident Evil. Little did he know that this was one of the first survival horror games with jump scares. When a dog broke through the window to chomp down on my video game character, Barney almost shit his pants. I have seen six-year old's jump less than this 20-year-old man. The weed had made him paranoid and he was headed for a bad trip. I was about to make it worse.

I looked out the hallway and saw something of interest. The house vacuum. This vacuum had lasted about 20 years or so in this animal house. This was seriously an old school beast that required fixing every week. The nice thing was that it was loud as hell and had a ginormous headlight on the front of it. I gave Barney the PlayStation paddle to let him to try out the game. I then slipped out to the bathroom and took a quick wiz. When I was on my way back, I grabbed the vacuum out of Barney's view and plugged that bad boy in. I could tell he was still in a jumpy mood because he was yelling at my TV screen and his game character. I brought the vacuum right to the edge of the door and turned it on about a foot or so away from him sitting on my couch.

I had just expected him to yelp a little as the noise would probably startle him in his heightened state. What I was not prepared for was for him to not only yell like a frightened kid and jump on the couch, but to go into attack mode. He knew it was me driving the vacuum towards him, he could see that close. Yet for some reason his brain rationalized that this was a monster and he needed to defend himself. He flew off the couch, but not at me. He deliberately drop kicked the vacuum.

At that point I was laughing my ass off, but I couldn't help but continue to provoke him. He was now wrestling the vacuum in the middle of the hall. He literally had it in a headlock. I pounced on him and got him away from trying to kill the poor machine. It was still running though, albeit with a much larger sound. So, I whipped it around and literally started chasing him like I was going to suck him up. He was too quick for my Nimbus 3000. He was just out of reach.

I noticed Jake was sitting up on top of the third-floor stairs, blazed out of his mind. But being thoroughly entertained by one idiot chasing another idiot around and both screaming like two 10-year olds.

That's when Barney pulled the unexpected. He jumped over the vacuum and kicked me in the chest, knocking me backwards and on my ass. In one swift move straight out of the World Wrestling Federation, he picked up old Bertha and raised it above his head and body slammed that poor old machine. After 20 years that was what finally ended that vacuum's life. It now sat in pieces.

Barney was a man possessed. He wanted more death. Jake had high-tailed back up the stairs and locked himself in his room. I ran quickly past Barney and got to my door when I realized Barney's death stare was directed right at me. While I knew we were possibly still playing around I wasn't about to take my chances. I slammed my door and got the deadbolt locked just in time for Barney to crash into my wooden door, cracking one of the upper door panels. This boy was dead set on getting into my room and killing his next monster. Me.

As we yelled at each other through the door, I realized he was not going to stop. Just as I backed away from the door, I heard the unmistakable splintering of my door coming off its hinges. It was now hanging on its hinges and the door frame was barely keeping it up. Now it was my turn to get pissed.

I yelled at Barney to get ahold of himself and oddly it worked. The weed paranoia seemed to dissipate, and the normal look came back into his eyes. As his sister's mixtape was playing "Runaway Train" by Soul Asylum I just did the only thing I could think of. When you can't beat them, join them. I started into a wild rage and ripped my door off its broken frame and threw it past Barney. He then joined me in jumping on the door out on the landing and reducing it to splinters.

I think it was when I realized I twisted my foot that I finally stopped, and Barney did too. He was on the ground doing his best cry laugh. I was right there with him. In that second floor landing it looked like a bomb went off. Machine parts scattered everywhere, and wood splinters and boards intertwined with the other wreckage. We both figured that was about enough for the night and it was time to retire and get some rest.

We would clean up the next day. I threw Barney's newly made mixtape at him and told him to beat it. He needed to go have some wine and chil-lax. He readily agreed, mumbling some sort of thanks for the mixtape for his sister.

The next morning, I was woken by our mutual friend Glen. He was somewhat laughing, but also a little pissed. The landing was a mess and we now had no vacuum to clean up the mess. When he asked me what happened I simply told him that Barney needed a gift for his sister and then things really went downhill from there. That's when Barney rolled down in his shower robe with his shower caddy. He just laughed and said that I needed to get dressed. He and I were headed to Sears to get a new vacuum and then to a lumber store to pick up a new door. We would be splitting that bill.

$300 each and about three hours later we had a new vacuum for the house and a new door for my room.

Worst. Mixtape. Ever.

THE ONE WITH THE NEW GIRL

Marriage is a very interesting transition in life. There are so many new elements added to your daily routine. So many other considerations to be wary of. You are truly taking on a partner in crime. If you really listen and put in effort it can pay off in dividends. So many twists and turns and if you enjoy the ride, instead of being sick on the ride, then it will be the ride of your life.

Then there is marriage with me. Which comes with a lot of baggage. Mainly my longtime friends. Thankfully, my wife has at least forgiven a good portion of my idiotic decisions and embraced my flawed, yet lovable, tribe of hooligans. The good news is that if I made a terrible decision, it always paled in comparison to the choices my friends made. Sadly, my wife was usually there and witnessed those decisions first hand. Probably too many times. But no one is counting here. This is not a competition.

The year was 2000. The Y2K bug had failed to emerge as humanity's next downfall. Smooth by Rob Thomas featuring Santana was blazing the charts. *Deuce Bigalow, Male Gigolo* was a hit at the box office. It was the best of times, it was the worst of times. Multiple generations trying to figure out how to navigate a new millennium.

Ava was not impressed. No, not with the way the world was going; she was not impressed with me. For the prior three months she had the baby of her nightmares. Nope, not our son. He was still 14 years away. She had a huge giant baby, me. I had the pleasure of breaking the first bone in my entire life. I went big for my first break. Broke my tibia and fibula with an amazing clean break. I had a hairline fracture in my jaw in high school, and that sucked. But this was a whole new, awful experience. Super lucky for me that I was married and super unlucky for my wife that she was married to me. Only that time. Maybe one other time.

** Oh. My. God. This was so painful, for me. He could not move at all. I had to dress him, bathe him, wrap his leg, and drive 30 minutes from my job every day at lunch to buy him Taco Bell. He is so lucky this was early in our marriage and I still wanted to take care of him. Not that I don't care now, but now I know what childbirth and living with a difficult child who didn't sleep for three years feels like. My sympathy threshold is way lower. **

I was basically a sack of shit for the first two months. Work let me stay at home and work remotely as much as possible. My business partner and other friends in the office would pick up the slack. It was the least my work could do since I broke my leg at their stupid ass company softball game. Thankfully, the medication helped ease my pain. Well, that and the new Dreamcast gaming system my wife had bought me was also dulling the pain. Unfortunately for my wife, we only had one TV at the time. I did make time to watch some Friends and West Wing during our together time. Just so she didn't have to watch me play Dreamcast all day. She took great care of me though.

When we got into month three and I was becoming more mobile and forced back into my cubicle, life started to ease up for her. I was less of an invalid and more of a somewhat mobile dependent. She was beginning to see some light at the end of the tunnel. I could sense my patient time was quickly coming to an end.

*Yes, this was probably the first difficult obstacle in our marriage. I was so ready for him to be back to normal and go back to work. In retrospect, it wasn't that disastrous. Life has a gentle way of easing you into hardship. At 24 this was tough, at 40 it would have been but a blip. My 40-year-old self could explain to my 24-year-old self what the hard stuff really looks like. *

When Labor Day rolled around, we needed to get out of Dodge, which was really Sacramento. We were not wealthy by any means, but we were always resourceful. Many of my close friends lived six hours south in the Los Angeles area. We lived too far away from family and flights into the remote lands that our family lived in was stupid expensive. So, driving it was much easier. After a couple of calls we figured out a way to have some fun with our friends and keep it well within our limited budget.

Unfortunately for my wife, that meant a weekend with George, Frank, and Dick. The good news for my wife was pouring like rain in a Milli Vanilli video. She only had to spend a single night in the Cucamonga with the four of us and then she got to move on to lovely Palm Springs. I was also starting to walk at this point. A little ahead of schedule, but I could not walk major distances yet. Still, things were all heading the right direction for my wife, and a vacation to a new place was welcomed.

*A weekend in Palm Springs sounded delightful. The boys would be there to entertain, and I would still have my own hotel room. Which was a big deal back then because everyone was still about saving money and sharing rooms. *

When we got into northern Los Angeles, it was already night. So, we went straight out. I needed some help from time to time to get around, but we mostly cabbed it. Ava was having fun and she got even more good news. She usually was the lone girl at most of our get togethers. This time though, Frank had a new girlfriend. Frank told Ava that she would not be the only girl. He was bringing his new girlfriend and was really excited for Ava to meet her. My friends loved Ava. Moreover, they respected her opinion when it came to their possible soulmates. So, Ava had that awesome ability going for her. She would finally have some estrogen around to offset the massive amount of testosterone that usually dominated her parties.

*I was very excited to meet the new girlfriend. Girlfriends generally moved in and out of everyone's lives quickly. But I always had hope that one might stick around for a little while. *

George had developed an unfortunate addiction to being single that would last him well into his 40s when he finally found the love of his life. Frank was a tank. Literally. Dude would always tell everyone that he could bench a 1978 Volkswagen Beetle. Never saw it, but I think he was more of a Mini Car type of bencher. That's my two cents. Dick, well, he was just an odd duck. He was older than us by a few years. He grew up in the wilds of Glacier Park and didn't have much city folk sensibility about him. He was still Montana plaid in a silk and satin busting metropolis. Dick had been in the pledge class at our fraternity with George and Frank. He was also now rooming with George and Frank in the Cucamonga. He did have his funny moments though. He was a welcome addition to the party.

*These three guys are ridiculous. But they are truly some of the kindest, most loyal individuals I have ever had the privilege of knowing. They are rough around the edges. And even though I bemoan their antics to this day, I love them. *

We slept in a little and went to brunch before departing on our two-hour journey to Palm Springs. We would meet Frank's new friend there. Of course, we screwed off on the drive. While Dick was the sober driver role, I took over permanent DJ role. Frank and George both claimed beer bully. My poor wife was listening to the same fucking stories she'd heard over, and over, and over again.

By the time we got to the outer city limits of Palm Springs, most of us had a good buzz going. I admit this is not socially acceptable in anyway. We were all fresh out of college and were still learning how to be grownups. In George's case, he graduated literally a year prior. He was on the Tommy Boy seven-year plan, but with no doctorate. He enjoyed his college experience to the max and utilized the many years learning about as much as his semester workload would allow. We all had limited expense budgets, so the accommodations were questionable. My wife was happy though, we had our own room, instead of her bunking with a bunch of guys which was the usual.

We got settled in and met Frank's new friend at the hotel bar. She seemed fun and down for a good weekend, so everything was looking up. I was chatting with the front desk lady and told her where we were from and that we wanted to know where to go to this weekend. She said the bars would be busy enough, but she only knew of one party that everyone seemed to be mentioning and buying tickets for. She said she didn't know much about it but if we went over to the Marriott's front desk, we could buy tickets and get more info. Let me remind you that this was way before any type of cell phone that worked on the internet. This was also way before Yelp or Facebook Events pages. The real wild west of partying. Take a person's suggestion on what's happening that night and then run with it.

We hailed a cab and headed the 10 or so miles to the suggested party. When we got to the lobby, we heard some tunes booming from the back of the hotel, around the pool area. This party was looking up. We should have taken the odd face the front desk lady gave us as the six of us walked in. We asked her about the party. She told us the tickets were $90 each and that included our alcohol and entertainment for the entire time we stayed at the event. While steep, we all realized there might not be much else going on. We all ponied up the cash and headed to the back of the hotel. Little did we know what the next 12 hours would entail for all of us.

When we rolled out into the huge ass pool party, we were met with skeptical looks. What the front desk manager had failed to tell us was that it was Latino Fest 2000. It was just billed as a normal pool party, but it was anything but that. My wife and Frank's new girlfriend gave each other a knowing sideways glance. There were a few half naked girls already bouncing around the pool. There was also a huge impromptu rave going on all around the pool. We were the only white people amongst the 300 or more party goers. The only thing that was missing was the DJ to scratch the song playing and every single person to look at us as we entered. Luckily most of the party goers were too deep into their own party really notice the six whitest people sauntering in.

We were not about to waste our well spent money. Even with the many sideways glances as we strolled through the rave, we knew we were getting some drinks. After a short wait, we got our cocktails and found our way to some chairs near the back of the party. This party was overbooked. There was zero room to get into the pool and the ladies were not buzzed enough to belly up to the naked party going on inside the pool. We downed our first drinks while enjoying this new world. While we quickly determined that we were going to make a quick exit, we needed to finish up the shots we had ordered. We were quickly pushed into party mode.

** This was a very unexpected experience. Everyone around us was having a fabulous time. The music was loud, and the drinks were flowing. While it was super uncomfortable having everyone stare at us, no one said anything inappropriate or rude to any of us. They were all quite welcoming and just let us be. **

As we exited, George had a request of us. He had packed in a hurry and had not brought the right clothes for the nicer dinner and clubbing that we were planning on doing that night. He wanted us to head to the downtown area of Palm Springs and help him find a nice shirt. He was also specific, he needed a Tommy Bahama brand island shirt. His belly needed to breath and he wanted to be a little more dressed up. We obliged and said we could look as well and stop in any bars we saw along the way to keep the party headed north.

A short cab ride later we were near a bunch of outdoor shops and plenty of options to keep the good vibes flowing. George was a man possessed. He was infatuated with Tommy Bahama and what it did to his overall party confidence. We probably went through seven stores before the golden goose laid its egg. In the back of a men's apparel shop was a lone Tommy Bahama section. George had found his Ark of the Covenant. Two hundred dollars lighter in his wallet George was now in official over the top party mode. We even got shots of tequila at the men's store while we waited on George to get his special shirt purchase tailored. We were ready to sit back and relax from the few miles George had us traversing. I was also nursing my leg as this was one of the longest physically taxing walks on my newly mended leg that I had done without crutches. We found a bar that was just opening for the day, so we all ducked in.

The bar was great, it was long but big. It also had a single stage near the back. We became friendly with the local bartender and asked their opinion of what to do on this busy weekend night. We also inquired if there was some local talent playing their stage that night. She let us know the places that were doing large dances and told us that they had world class Karaoke going on. She told us we should come back after dinner and before we headed to one of the many parties going on. We finished up another round and determined it was time to go back to the rooms and get ready for dinner. We were staying above the bell curve in the inebriated department.

The oddest thing started to happen though. Frank was starting to get to his tipping point. We noticed this on the shopping spree. He was also being a little dismissive to his new date partner. Nothing disrespectful, just not very attentive. By the time we were finishing up at the world-famous Karaoke bar, we also took notice that Dick was coming out of shell a little more than usual. He was making some sweet jokes and genuinely in a heightened state of bliss. He wasn't even doing any drugs to attain that charming level. We also took note of Frank's girlfriend taking note of Dick's witty humor. We all concluded that it was just because Frank was a little over the limit on his drinking game. He was starting to get to that rage in the cage type of drunkenness. Which with big Frank could go so many directions. The good news was that Frank and his new girl were headed back to their room and could sort out their business before we headed back out to dinner.

By the time we all met up in the lobby for dinner, my freshly fixed leg was throbbing. The constant moving, looking for George's 'must have style of the 60's' and our Latin friends' rave, it was overworked. The good news was that the last of my pain pills were working and I could relax a little bit and have some good conversations with everyone. Right away we saw that Dick was way overdressed. He even had on a massive amount of Drakkar Noir. We also felt a little bit of cold coming from Frank and his girlfriend of seven days. No worries. We already had plans in place to keep the party moving in an even better direction.

When we were dropped off a few miles away at our extravagant dinner at Dick's Last Resort we saw that even though we were trying to avoid too many lines this holiday weekend, we were not getting away with it. Frank the Tank was on fire. He was batting at all the good personal jokes. Unfortunately, his new friend was not enamored by his brilliance. So as soon as we got to the front desk to check in for our reservation, Frank grabbed George and secreted him to the back of the restaurant. That seemed to work out for the moment as the rest of us sat the few minutes to wait for our table to clear. Sure enough, there seemed a vibe between Frank's gal and Dick. Even my wife was now picking up on it. We blew it off and our table was cleared, and we were headed into a little bit of sobriety. Or so we thought.

Since Frank and George were nowhere to be seen for the next ten minutes, the four of us started off with a drink and a shot, courtesy of Frank's new friend. When George came back to the table by himself, we chided him a little bit and then asked where his bodyguard was. He said Frank was having a "moment" and he would be with us shortly. We didn't realize that meant that Frank was heaving up some Mezcal that he and George had just partaken in. We ordered without Frank and kept the jovial vibe rolling.

When our food arrived, Frank still had not managed his way back to our table and his girlfriend was done. She expressed her disappointment that her date had ditched her, and she was contemplating leaving that night to go back to Temecula. We all convinced her to stay. That she was welcome even if our friend was engaged in his usual triangle arm-bar lock in across the restaurant. She agreed and luckily Dick was there to comfort her.

*I will admit, I was furious with Frank. He was being so incredibly rude to his guest. We were doing everything we could to make her feel comfortable. Also, a little clarification, we waited over two hours for our table. I know because I was starving. I don't do well when I'm hungry. When Frank finally sat down to join us, and I was already mad, he started eating off my plate. His drunk ass had not been there to order and now he was eating my food! I was not having it. I was not too kind. I picked up my plate and walked to the other end of the table. *

Frank finally barged in. He made some grumbling sounds that re-sembled an apology for taking so long. His new date took him aside and had some words with him. Frank apparently agreed, and all things were right with the night. It was time to get our cab. We headed back to the world-famous karaoke bar. Time to up the bet.

As we were deposited in front of our next destination, we noticed that there was a little older clientele. It was also packed. We got in quick enough, but we had to sit quite a few rows back to watch the performances.

We apparently ended up at one of the premier karaoke spots in the United States. The girls were blown away by the next few performances they watched. The guys were perplexed as why these singers brought their own costumes to perform in. Back home at our Karaoke bars ev-erything was singing and performance. Sometimes performance out-weighed the singing, especially in our experiences.

It came as no surprise that our friends', Frank and George, names were called. As they drunkenly tried to get the rest of us up to the stage, we saw the entire audience watch with bated breath to see what these two loud men were about to perform for them. Those two couldn't wrangle any of us to the stage. Frank's girlfriend looked like she wanted to run out of the place. Dick was there to tell her to watch the show. This performance was going to make up for the past few hours.

When the opening words of my buddies' karaoke song choice came on, Dick, my wife, and I all looked at each other and nodded in agreement that this was about to get good. They were singing their favorite duet, "American Pie" by Don McLean. They had sung this tune in the past in front of many fortunate bar patrons across the United States. There was even some early clapping and shouts of approval as the music and lyrics first hit. Then it got weird.

The amount of booze consumed earlier that day, and the whiskey courage shots they took right before jumping on stage, kicked in right at that moment where they were starting their own little concert. What normally would have been a "B" grade karaoke attempt turned into a full-blown house of horrors. We all knew something was off when George and Frank started by doing the good old one arm, side by side hug and sway to start off their singing masterpiece. Then their memory of the lyrics began to fade quickly. Now in these two knuckleheads' defense, they had probably sung this particular song with one another no more than a dozen times in the past 8 or so years. Also, in their defense, they probably were not normally as inebriated as they were this night.

The train wreck was starting and there was zero heading back. For the five of us in the back of the bar we could only try to duck our heads and pretend that we did not know the two guys bellowing out death metal on stage. To say they were out of tune would be a disrespect to people who try to sing but are just a bit off. No, this sounded like a full-on shout fest to the crowd, with all the moves of those "entourage" homies that bounce around while the main rapper sings at a concert.

The best part was when the two-second sobriety point hit both of them at the same time and they realized the entire crowd was dead silent and had turned on them. They had two choices right then: either get off stage and say their fond farewells or spice up their act and try to salvage their performance. To our table's horror, and delight, they opted for option number two. At that point, they started yelling at the crowd to get involved. When that did not work, they upped it another level and went out to the front row of patrons and started handing them the mike to sing parts of their karaoke song. Then something happened that our group will have etched into our memories for the entirety of our lives. Frank and George were in full realization on how bad their performance was going.

They only had one more salvation move left. They decided that they would pick out a couple of the older regular ladies in the front row for a public exhibition of their incredible dancing moves. We all watched in horror as they each pointed to their lady of choice and slowly grind walked over to them and started to do a fully clothed male strip dance on these flabbergasted women. This became one of the group highlights in a long night. My wife might remember things a little differently, but I do remember these two recently retired ladies, while initially disgusted, ended up going with the flow. They reluctantly got up and did the Elaine dance with the boys as well as screamed with Frank and George every time "American Pie" came over the speakers.

** This event was so humiliating, I still feel embarrassment for them almost 20 years later. I do believe this was the end of their public karaoke career. I do not remember any of the women they targeted being pleased in anyway. But maybe I'm just projecting. I do remember being incredibly thankful for the back table so* *that we could watch in terrified delight. A massive amount of wreckage that you just cannot look away from.* *

It was about this time that management and staff at the bar decided it was time to call it. I want to say, and this is generous, that they cut off Frank and George around the two thirds mark of the song. They literally walked up to them, sat the dancing ladies down, and grabbed their microphones. Not before George got off one last heavy metal laden "American Pie" shout out to the universe.

The bar managers quickly asked that our group settle the tab and then it was time to move on. I think they even comped some of our drinks for us getting Frank and George out as quickly as possible. George and Frank gave them hugs and high fives and said they would be back later that night. The bar managers only stared as they told them they were only joking, but that exit was a blur to this day. Luckily, the other 50 patrons in the bar got to see the kicking out of the worst karaoke singers they had met to date. If they only were able to see where this story would go in the next 12 hours.

By this time, Frank's date was really done. She was trying to figure out how to leave. Dick interceded and told her that it couldn't go downhill from here. My wife even reiterated that point that this was just par for the course when this group gets together, and the worst should be behind her. Besides, they were not married and had only recently begun to see each other. So at least take part in the vacation weekend party and enjoy what she could. Somehow that worked. She stayed with us to the bitter end.

George and Frank were tore up at this point. Not saying the rest of us were not beyond our best moments but they were beyond the place with the pines. We asked some people walking by where the party was at, because we were flying blind. They said they were heading down to a local club that had some big DJ and that it should be crazy busy. We followed right behind them. George and Frank were in the back of the pack doing the ceremonial hug walk talking about old times and friendship. Frank was barely able to keep normal walk about him.

When we got to the line for the club it was literally out the door and stretching out to the street. But we tagged along with the people who told us about it, and they got us up to the other side. They apparently knew someone who knew someone. And we knew them, for all of 10 minutes. The problem was Frank. He was starting to get hot from the walk and he really wanted to take off his shirt. We all tried to keep that from happening, and we thought we had done a good job, but then the bouncers told us the bad news. They saw Frank wobbling up to the line and using their fine-tuned judgement they pre-determined that he probably was not fit to head into the packed club. To this day I have no clue what we said that changed their mind. They were 100% correct on Frank but they missed that the rest of us that were also over the line. I think that was the ladies and Dick's determination to get dancing in on this long day. Either way we all held up Frank past security and up the stairs to the final party.

It was the right party to be at during this long parade of a day. The place was packed but not to the point of saturation. Pretty sure we walked into Mystikal's "Shake Ya Ass" as we came through the door. Even the lines to get into the bar were short. I told the group I would grab them a round and I just needed someone with me to carry the drink back. My wife hastily agreed. As we got our order, and both picked up the drinks we realized we lost track of where the rest of our group was.

We slowly walked out to the dance floor. What we saw next should have made sense all the way around. But my wife and I kept finding ourselves hitting each other as we found the remnants of our original group.

My wife spotted George right away. When she hit me and pointed to his general vicinity, I was greeted with something our group affectionately dubbed "rage in the cage". George had a propensity to find a ledge, or stage at any club, and decided that the crowd needed to check out his amazing "arm way up in the air" dance. There was George, in all his Tommy Bahama tropical shirt glory, hanging from a small handful of curtains behind him. He was barely able to get both of his feet on the ledge he was one arm upping from. The funny part was, he had six other people on that ledge next to him. He couldn't Ava or me, but we got to experience that joy first hand.

It was about then that I spotted Frank. He was nowhere near George. He was more towards the back of the bar while George was ledge dancing near the front. But what made me hit my wife's arm harder to grab her attention to what was going on with Frank. When my wife turned around, she damn near dropped her slew of drinks. To be fair, we could not just look across the bar and see Frank. No. The only way we could see him and know it was him was there was a huge mirror above the pool tables in the back. And we could clearly see Frank, surrounded by three little hot Asian ladies. The reason my wife almost dropped her drinks though was the fact that he was standing there with no shirt. Somehow in the few minutes it took for the group to separate, Frank thought because it was so hot outside that he could take his shirt off inside the temperature-controlled club. Funny enough the ladies he was talking to seemed enamored by his half nakedness. They were laughing with him and he seemed happy as could be. We decided that we would take his drink, he was probably good.

Then my wife got in the last jab. She elbowed me hard and yelled into my ear. She had found Dick as well as Frank's previous girlfriend. They were in the middle of the dance floor, just outside George's peripheral sight and somewhat blended into the ever-increasing throng of party goers. They were also doing the 8th grade middle school slow dance all the while OutKast was blasting in the background. This was a trio of sights in a very short amount of time.

My wife dropped off drinks to each person in our party. Except for Frank. She did not want his new girlfriend to see his random nakedness situation going on over on the other side of the club. My wife grabbed me and took me out to the dance floor. We tried our best to blend into the party and let the other people in our group to go about their owns paths. Shortly after Ava and I started our dancing George danced his way back to us. He was super excited about something. He told us that he had just found Dick making out with Frank's weekend date. He advised that we should get out of the club while we could and call it a night. We wanted nothing to do with a possible fight coming about between two close friends. We quickly agreed with George and poured out of the club, quickly saying our goodbyes to the rest of the group.

Outside my booze wore off and the crisp night air snapped me back to reality. I was on my second week of walking on my newly recovered leg. I had been working it out all day and now it was done. I literally was at a place where my leg was done with me and was not going to cooperate with our plans to walk back to the hotel. So, we walked out front and tried desperately to look for a cab. Again, the days before smartphones and a proliferation of Uber drivers was defiantly against us. There were no cabs available. We waited around about a half hour and did not see one in our vicinity. George was my crutch on the short walk to breakfast.

My wife helped where she could, but it mainly fell on George. Luckily, he only had a partial workout with the ledge dancing that night and he had enough energy to drag me to breakfast. Sadly, after we left breakfast, he had to piggyback me the rest of the way to the hotel. But as friends do, we help when the chips are low. Just ask Dick.

That next morning, we woke up to some searing heat coming through our bedroom window. I also heard some people talking right outside our hotel door. I figured I had better get up and at least check to see if I needed to say goodbye to Frank and his newly single girlfriend. I peeked out the window and was surprised to see Dick out on the front porch with Frank's hours old ex-girlfriend. They kissed, hugged, and she got in her car and drove off. At that point I realized that Dick had just successfully swooped Frank's girlfriend of the weekend. I'm sure he was super worried knowing that he and Frank were about to have a very un-comfortable ride back to the Inland Empire. My wife laughed when I told her what just happened. This was pretty much par for the course in her life with my dumbass friends.

When the rest of us got up and got our travel bags packed, we headed to our car to make the long haul back west. As predicted, Frank and Dick were not as animated towards each other as they normally would have been. That said there was an underlying understanding. As it turned out, those new la-dies that Frank had met, with his shirt off, ended up being a better match for him than his past girlfriend. While the bro code had been broken, there were very rare acceptable common-sense actions that were being accepted.

Before everyone could get comfortable in the very cramped backseat of our little Honda Accord, we had one more errand to run. As it turned out both George and Frank had woken up next to each other in their room and as they recalled the stories from the night before, they realized they were both missing their debit cards. Before we could go back to the IE, we had the joy of retracing our unfortunate steps of the previous night.

We only found one of the two lost cards. Sadly, that one was found at the scene of the karaoke crime. Also, super lucky for our entire party was the fact that the bartender and waitress on duty remembered us right away. As they graciously explained that George had a large tip automatically added to his final bill, they also decided that we should relive the horror that their customers experienced. American Pie it was not. The crème of the corn of that disturbing conversation was when they brought over to the main bar area and showed us the broken bookshelf. My wife and I were confused as to why they were showing us this.

They then described to our group that when Frank and George were done with their strip tease, they came back to the bar and attempted to order themselves some shots of Old Crow whiskey. When they were instead asked to leave, Frank, with all his 280 plus pound frame, somehow decided that that bookshelf would make a great place to sit. Oddly enough, that bookshelf didn't hold, and we were looking at the splinters that were still all over the bar floor. Which was sad because it looked to be an older bookshelf and a one of a kind.

It was then that the world decided to elaborate on its description of this cosmic event. George yelled aloud which startled everyone in proximity. He just saw the mandatory gratuity that was added to his final bill. He was now the proud owner of an expensive pile of wood.

At least he had his $200 Tommy Bahama shirt that he scored from Palm Springs. Silver hair lining in everything no matter the situation. Positive thoughts people.

** Chances version above and my version are the same. Entertaining. Memorable. Never repeating. **

IT'S A SMALL WORLD AFTER ALL

I was sitting down at a new pub that I had just discovered in the back streets of Laramie, Wyoming. I was staying the night for my day job and I had a stay over for appointments in the morning. I like visiting local watering holes when I am traveling in new towns. I love the energy I get from them. Usually it is where I find my inspiration to write. I sit down in a crowded bar and start writing amongst the noise and chaos. I'm sure it's my ADHD.

This bar in that foreign, yet familiar town, would not disappoint when it came to bring a spark to my creativity.

The name of the establishment was what initially caught my eye. Then I saw a few people sitting at the quaint bar and I doubled back and walked in. Born in the Barn was the catalyst for this story. Chris Fairbanks was the final straw that made it all happen.

As I sat down, the bartender offered me a beer menu that was chock full of plenty of options for food. I was just in time for happy hour. A couple of younger guys sat to the left of me and then a couple and their friends sat to my right. Almost all the dinner tables were empty. It was a slow night in this generally bustling college town. It was a Wednesday night and it felt like -29 degrees outside. In fact, it was a pretty warm one for Laramie this late into January. It was one out of the nine nights a year that was void of howling wind. Things were looking up.

I ordered the bartender's recommendation for a local craft beer and his favorite dish. As I was sipping my freshly served brew and waiting for my wings to come out, one of the guys to my immediate left looked over at me and made a comment about the biting cold. I agreed. Then we both said we had experienced even colder weather in Laramie. A quick handshake later we were chatting about random things. I generally would have been a little irritated as I was trying to get this book written. I was up against my own self-imposed deadline. However, this younger dude was interesting and had some interesting stories to tell.

He was a professional bull rider and he had recently moved to Laramie with his older brother. They were both from Texas. His brother had been riding in the PRCA for five more years than he had. This is a call back to my previous book. In "Hang 'em High" I wrote about one of my sister's ex-husbands insane stories from Texas. I asked this young buck if he knew Hambone. Sure as shit, his eyes lit up and he said that of course he did. His records were still in the PRCA hall of fame. He and his brother didn't know him personally, but they sure knew who he was and his legend.

I love catching those random stranger moments when the world seems a lot smaller. So, as we chatted, I told him I had a hell of a story to tell him. It was about the time that my sister and I possibly ran from death himself, and how death ended up on my mom's operating table. The opening chapter in my last book. That's when some sort of weird fate played its cards. As I was around the middle of the story, I happened to avert my eyes to the TV above me. No real reason, nothing was on. Yet as my eyes focused on the commercial, I squinted a bit as if to connect what my brain was really telling me. There, in his full curly hair and professional mustache glory was a friend of mine from high school. You couldn't miss Chris Fairbanks even if you didn't know him.

As I told my new stranger friend that I was distracted from the story I was recanting, he looked up to watch the 30 second H&R Block commercial with me. Yup, it was Fairbanks. I had been to four of his stand-up shows in various cities that I happened to live. I had also seen him start to gain media attention. He had been on Conan and Kimmel. He also competed on The Last Comic Standing on NBC back in its heyday. Chris had even recently shown up in some random shows that I was watching on HBO and Comedy Central. He was doing what he had set out to do. He was succeeding. I am sure that spot for H&R paid a couple of days of rent in SoCal. Rent down there is no joke. Yet Chris' jokes and acting career were getting brighter and brighter each time I ran across him. Far from the very first time I saw one of his professional comedy shows.

I finished up my dinner and bid my new friend a good night. I had an early work meeting the next day. Before I hit the bed to rack out, I sent my wife a quick good night text. I also sent her the YouTube link to the commercial I just saw with my old friend in it. She was always the first person I would show when I ran across Chris' media stuff. She laughed and said it was nice to see him doing so well. It was a far cry from her first experience with Chris.

I decided to post a random Facebook message to Chris' page. Sure, it had been a minute since we had seen each other or spoken with one another, but that didn't mean we couldn't catch up. I let him know I had just seen his commercial. I also told him I had heard his podcast partner

Karen's other podcast where she had retold the story of the same serial killer in our hometown of Missoula that I had started to tell the rodeo dude. Chris and Karen's podcast called "Do You Need A Ride." After I sent the post I was out like a light.

It was to my surprise in the morning I had some new notifications. They were for that shithole social media site that we are all still glued to for some reason. When I looked, I saw a couple of my high school buddies liked my post on Chris' timeline last night. I had almost forgotten I had posted it.

However, Chris had written a post back to me. He said he was happy to see this post and that it was random that I had written to him. He hadn't heard from me in a while. As it turned out he had just mentioned me on his "Do You Need a Ride" podcast. He told me only that he had mentioned the night I randomly surprised him on one of his first stand-up shows.

It's probably about time to address the elephant in the room. No, I am not talking about my slight love of a couple of delicious craft beers here and there. I inherited that taste straight from my father, although he is a Scotch fan, not beer. Not my mother. I should probably point that out again, as it will make my mom's day when she reads this. No, I am talking about the first Fairbank's comedy show that my wife and I attended that Chris mentioned in his podcast.

I remember being stuck in bumper to bumper traffic on Sunrise Fucking Boulevard, during my tortuous two-hour commute home. I was listening to the local rap station and on came a barrage of ads. Generally, I would have switched to my mixed CDs I had, but the first ad happened to be for our larger comedy venue. I wanted to see who was playing that weekend.

My wife and I absolutely loved going to shows on the weekends. We had the pleasure of seeing some very early acts of now major Hollywood stars. Names like Dave Chappelle, Gabriel Iglesias, Karen Kilgariff, Whitney Cummings, and the unforgettable Mitch Hedberg. We were fortunate to see so many comics at the beginning of their careers. It was our date night tradition. It still would be if we didn't have those fucking kids. Kidding. Totally kidding. I love to stay home on Friday nights and watch PJ Masks on repeat. It's the best.

As I heard the headliner for the weekend, I was stoked. He was an unknown to me, which meant that the tickets would be cheaper, which meant I got at least one more "special juice." That was my nickname I gave Long Island Iced Teas. My wife hated when I ordered them like that to our waitress and she had to explain what the real drink name was. It was my tiny form of sit-down comedy. The headliner was some dude named Daniel Tosh. Then they named off the other comedians before the headliner. The other guy was someone I didn't know either, which was a good sign. While celeb stand-ups had a very polished act and were reliably funny, the up and coming gals and guys generally went all out. No boundaries, which made their acts even that much funnier.

When they got to the third name, my ADHD that was generally running at a 100% level dropped to like 11%. The name they dropped was none other than Chris Fairbanks, my old friend from high school and my early skateboarding days. I hadn't seen Chris in about 8 or 9 years since we graduated. There was also no way that there was some other dude out there named Chris Fairbanks. I was perplexed but also super excited.

I got home 30 minutes later than usual thanks to some D bag that decided to park his Honda Accord on the back of a Toyota Corolla near the Citrus Heights Mall. It didn't matter though. I was excited to tell Ava that we were headed down to Punch Line comedy club. I told her I had found out there was a good chance that we would be in for a fun surprise: a friend of mine from Missoula would be playing before the headliner. It was a no brainer, so Ava got herself all fancy and I started sucking down some suds. My wife excelled in sober driving back in the day.

When we got to the club entrance the line had already started to form. Which was nothing new as the 200-seat venue was usually sold out. That night turned out to be no different. The good news for me was that we got there in time to be near the front of the line. The bad news for my wife was that we got there in time to be in the front of the line. Ava absolutely hated when we were seated in the front row. Every single time I would be the one the comic would single out. I was easy bait, and I loved every second of it. Sometimes though when I had that one extra "special juice" I would want to interact with said comedian which usually meant our table was spotlighted for the night. Ava wants to sit in the shadows and enjoy the moment, she hates the spotlight and public interaction. So, every single time the host would ask us our party size and I said it was just my wife and I, we would generally then be asked if we were ok with being sat in the front row. I cordially replied yes, while Ava hit me on my back to try to let me know that she did not want to sit in the front row. In those days she had a very low winning percentage at comedy clubs.

That night was no different. We ended up in the front row. Which was great because the very first comedian up was none other than the one and only Chris Fairbanks. To be fair, I did not research that last statement. There might be more "one and only" Chris Fairbanks. But to me, this was the one and only. He looked just like he did when I last saw him in high school.

When he came out, he started with his general hellos and normal awkward bravado. I could tell he had a bit of nerves about him. Which led me to think that if for some reason he did happen to notice me, I would try to not throw him off with my presence. I just wanted to see an old buddy make the crowd move. I did not find out, until recently listening to his successful podcast, that he had a very bad drinking stage of life. That was lost on me because I was already one "special juice" down.

Sure enough, he took a step back when our eyes locked and he seemed to realize who I was. At that point he was already starting his set and noticing me did exactly what I did not want it to do. A distraction and a detour.

Right away Chris asked me if I was who he thought I was. I immediately told him no. He was confused but decided to go with it. Yet he took it another route. One that I absolutely loved, but the other 199 people in the room, including Ava, did not follow. He went on a comedic rampage about this buddy he knew and hated in high school. That buddy was me. He went on to describe my unfortunate follies that happened during that period in our lives. He described to the crowd how this asshat named Chance had his jaw broken by one of his good friends. He then thought it was hilarious that almost two weeks later this Chance character happened to be going to a popular off school site after school to watch a big fight that was supposed to go down. Chris then lambasted that poor Chance, to the absolute delight of myself, about how one of Chance's buddies ended up running him over in that popular fight spot that fateful day. These two facts were positively true. I had forgotten how close in proximity these two separate incidents were until early 2019.

Ava was not impressed. Mainly because I was rolling with laughter from Chris' bit. I thoroughly enjoyed my own private roast. When it was evident that the entire population of that room was done with this private joke, Chris sobered up enough to announce his good bye. He still had one more unplanned gift for the audience. He missed the first step as he was exiting the stage and fell down the side. To the audience, that was the best part of his bit. To me that was just the topper to the cake he had just presented me.

Then Tosh came on. Daniel absolutely slayed the mic that night. He went over by almost forty minutes and had the crowd in stitches.

I felt terrible for Chris after watching his performance. To the 199 in the room he had bombed beyond belief. He also had the misfortune to lead one of the best up and coming comedians in the game at that time. Tosh had a dream night for his profession. Those performances were what ended up getting Tosh his own Comedy Central show, which then blew up. It then came full circle and featured Fairbanks in an odd skateboarding bit, something I randomly caught one night and the first person I was able to tell? My wife. Something, something, time is a flat circle or something like that? Alright, alright, alright.

When everyone was filing out after the club announced closing, I held Ava back. I told her I wanted to stop by and at least chat with Chris. It was the least I could do. Sure enough Chris was in the back bar, drink in hand, and waiting for me. He knew it was me. I told him that I was sorry to stop in on him unannounced. He apologized to my wife and me and told me it was all just a bit. I laughed it off as I had before. Ava was not so sure. She didn't know Chris and the very first time she met him he was shitting all over me. Which as any good target in a comedy show knows, never take it personally. I knew Chris was trying to get a rise from the crowd, he just didn't know he was only doing that bit for me. We hugged it out and went our separate ways. Never to talk about that weird night again until I heard his podcast that fateful cold February day of 2019 in Cheyenne, Wyoming.

Now to be fair, Chris had given me a heads up about the podcast on that Facebook post. It's when I heard the recent podcast that it sparked those glorious old memories. Sometimes we need to sort through the shit that is life to find that gold we had yesterday. Furthermore, sometimes we must clean that dust off to make us remember the shine our own gold really possessed. It sparked enough that I was not sure how to end this story and I was a mere two months out from my launch party in Missoula.

That one simple interaction was enough to supply a lifetime full of shit to part like the Red Seas. It gave me the clarity to make this book a complete circle. I have always pictured myself moving alone in a big, uncaring world. Seemingly meaningless interactions from long ago can be rediscovered 20 years later. It is a small world. We are all connected and part of one another's stories. This is what strengthens us. Never take life for granted. It will always give you what you need when you need it and show you the path.

Now what's your small world story?

#cheers

P.S.

I wanted to end with a cliffhanger like I did in my first book. I appreciate that so many people wrote to me and were very angry about me not finishing the story. I thought I would let all those people know that those comments were not ignored.

I guess what I am trying to say is that what Madame Vera said to me that fateful day, up in Estes Park, was the most shocking thing I had heard in my life. I believe that I have an obligation to live out her predictions.

I'm much better at seeing my path these days. I am also eternally grateful for her honesty and belief in me as a person and the person she believes I am destined to become.

Alas, this book has rambled on enough. I will leave details of that conversation for another chapter in a different book . . .

Dedication

This book is dedicated to my friends and family.

Without you there is no change. My nights and days are grey. If I reached out and touched the rain, it just wouldn't feel the same.

Naw. Just messing with you. That's totally the opening verse for Motley Crue's hit song "Without You." You should know me better by now. Let me try again.

Without you the pages in this book would be blank. Technically true if you are my parents.

What is also true is that each one of you that has graced my life in some way is responsible for creating this monster. I blame every one of you for the things I have done and for the things I can never un-see.

To my family: I am legally bound by United States law to share my surname with you. I am also bound by the laws of science to share my DNA with you. I am not bound to share anything past that. The reason

I still do share my life and come around so often isn't just because of the free place to stay while I am passing through. No, I do like you all and I love the rich history and terrible stories we all share together. You can go to prison, you can move far, far away, you can even try to die, but you will never lose me. Even though you try. I would say try harder, but we both know I still win that battle. Like a bad STD, I am with you forever. Hearts.

To my friends: You may come and go like the breeze, but you will always remember that one time with Chance. While I can't be held legally liable for that statement, I think we both know truth behind it. Without your love and support I would have never made this book. That's an absolute crock of shit. Let's try that again. Without your terrible ideas and peer pressure these stories would have never materialized. Sadly, you can't take that to the bank. Because you are not represented within these pages. Some dumb ghost author named Chance was told by his publisher to change the names of all involved to protect them from their mothers. True story bros. Hugs.

To my fans: I see all three of you! Thanks for spreading the good word about chance_the_author. I am currently trending nowhere on Twitter and am ranked 19,999,997th on Amazon's hot new authors list. You are doing good work out there from Mumbai and Nairobi. You out there in Kazakhstan? You could probably exert a tiny more energy into promoting me from your MySpace platform. I think Tom bought the book though. Congrats on getting that friend invested. Kisses.

I have always said my first book is dedicated to my children. This book is dedicated to my friends, family, and three fans. What about your wife,

Chance? No love? Easy amigos. Go back and read the acknowledgement section in the first book of this trilogy.

Don't worry. Book three is dedicated to only one person. Me. Kidding!

Of course, it will be dedicated to the wife. She's writing the other fucking half of book three. Cheers.

ABOUT THE AUTHOR

How about you just go buy my first book in this trilogy? You can't be that lazy, can you? My author intro is in the very back of that gem. I really don't think I need to repeat myself in this space. As you probably already read, I did a great job of babbling on and on and on and on and so forth. Oh. You are the type of person that reads this section to decide if you like what you read then you will buy the book? In that case here is the CliffsNotes then:

Age: Somewhere between 18 and 81.

Sex: Yes. Often. That's a lie. We have kids.

Married: Depends on the sales of this book.

Religion: Missio.

From: My mother's womb.

About: It's pronounced "Ah-boot" in Canada. Little fun fact for you.

Favorite Food: In N Out, Double-Double, Grilled Onions, Ketchup and Lettuce only. Animalized Fries.

Favorite Child: Trick question. The greatest trick the devil ever pulled was convincing the world he didn't exist.

Publisher's Note

You can find many interesting things about this author on his various social media sites he uses.

Please search the Gram (Instagram for you folks over 40) for: chance_the_author

You can search Reddit, Imgur and even Twitter for that same handle. You have been warned.

Author's Note

My publisher is a real asshole. I can't wait for the third book to come out so I can fire their ass.

Author's Wife's Note

We are out of wet cat food again. Chuck Norris is being a real dick. Can you pick some up on your way home from the Avanti? Also tell Greg Studley to stop leaving those sick voice messages on the phone recorder. We lost another housekeeper because she thinks our place is haunted. Love you!